SCIENCE, FAITH, AND ETHICS

SCIENCE, FAITH, AND ETHICS

GRID OR GRIDLOCK?

DENIS ALEXANDER &
ROBERT S. WHITE

HENDRICKSON
PUBLISHERS

Hendrickson Publishers, Inc.
P. O. Box 3473
Peabody, Massachusetts 01961-3473

Printed in the United States of America

First Printing — March 2006

Library of Congress Cataloging-in-Publication Data

Alexander, Denis.
    [Beyond belief]
    Science, faith, and ethics : grid or gridlock? / Denis Alexander and Robert S. White.
        p. cm.
    Originally published: Beyond belief. Oxford, England : Lion Hudson, c2005.
    Includes bibliographical references and index.
    ISBN 1-59856-018-2 (alk. paper)
    1. Civilization, Modern—1950– 2. Science and civilization.
  I. White, R. S. (Robert S.) II. Title.
    CB430.A43 2006
    909.82—dc22
                        2005035922

This book is dedicated to the next generation:

Christopher, Helen, Sheona, Sarah, Mark, and Sarah

Contents

Acknowledgments

We thank all those who have helped us clarify our thoughts, have straightened out our theology or our scientific understanding when necessary, and have pointed us to relevant publications. RSW particularly thanks Christopher Ash for his encouragement and support.

Preface

Have you ever played that party game where you have to say the first word that comes into your head, and it has to be the opposite of the previous word: "hot—cold"; "tall—short"; "man—woman"; "science—faith"? All too often, our unthinking reaction is that science and religious faith lie at opposite poles—the former objective, clinical, universal, rational; the latter subjective, emotional, personal, unprovable.

Or maybe, with fresh in your mind last night's TV images of the carnage surrounding the latest suicide bombing by a religious fanatic, or the despoliation resulting from another environmental catastrophe, you simply think "a plague on both your houses," put aside thoughts of both science and religion and try just to get on with your own life. So why are the two of us, both active scientists with fulfilling professional careers in fast-moving scientific fields, and both of us committed Christians, asking you to consider the interactions between science and faith?

One reason stems from our conviction that religious faith makes a big difference in the way we think about the world, not only in our private lives but also in the public domain where the scientific advances of the twenty-first century will continue to raise acute ethical issues. Ironically, just as science thought it was seeing religion out the back door, so it is now increasingly coming back in through the front door as the applications of science raise a plethora of moral questions that lie well beyond the ability of science itself to resolve.

In the first part of this book we look at what science is and what it can do, and then in a similar way we examine and critique a wide range of religious beliefs about why this world is the way it is. Next we consider what happens when science and faith meet. Our conclusions might be surprising to some—we find that science and Christian faith have a great deal in common in the way they view the material world and the way it works. Indeed, historically many leading and ground-breaking scientists have been Christians who saw a seamless connection between their science and their faith.

Science and Christianity share certain common assumptions about the difference between truth and untruth, fact and fiction, and in their belief in an ultimate reality which can be rationally investigated. In our contemporary society—influenced by relativism and its popular counterpart that "anything goes," with its lack of certainty in any absolutes—the shared stance of science and Christianity toward the search for reliable knowledge finds many resonances.

In the second part of the book we discuss some of the scientific issues that face humankind at the beginning of the twenty-first century. Among them are questions of the possibility of genetic modification of plants, of animals and even of humans. Does Christianity have anything distinctive to contribute to the ethical debate over genetically modified (GM) foods, assisted reproduction or cloning? Should some things be off-limits, even if scientifically feasible, simply because the risks are too high, or because they break ethical boundaries? And does Christianity have anything to contribute to the discussions over global climate change, cultural and economic globalization, or sustainable development and consumption?

One of us (DA) is a biological scientist, the other (RSW) a physical scientist. Between us we span a broad range of science. We have had a lot of fun debating the issues across our fields of specialization. But the debate is more than just academic. Humankind is now capable of manipulating genomes in ways that seemed impossible only a few decades ago. At the same time we are causing the extinction of species, global climate change and environmental modification at a rate never before experienced on earth.

Such issues are too important to leave to the specialists and a broad public debate is essential. That is why we have tried to avoid specialist language and to make this introductory overview as accessible as possible to a general readership. So whether you are a person of faith or of none, a scientist or an interested non-scientist, we invite you to consider the interactions between modern science and religious faith.

Part I

Science and Religion

CHAPTER 1

What's It All About?

Everyone knows what science is, until pressed to provide a definition: then they tend to become much more hazy. Part of the problem is that the meaning of the word itself has changed over the centuries. We may, for example, speak of "Greek science," referring to the science that flourished in ancient Greece and in centers such as Alexandria over the period 600 B.C.E. to 200 C.E., but the science of that era is a very distant cousin of the type of science practiced today. The modern scientific enterprise, complete with scientific societies, journals, specialized laboratories and distinct disciplines, did not really emerge until the sixteenth century onwards.

The word "scientist" was not even invented until the first half of the nineteenth century—by William Whewell (pronounced "Hule"), the polymath clergyman and Master of Trinity College, Cambridge. It seems fitting for the theme of this book that the word scientist was invented by an Anglican vicar! Up until that time practitioners of science were known as natural philosophers. In 1851 Charles Babbage complained that "Science in England is not a profession: its cultivators are scarcely recognized even as a class." It was not until the latter half of the nineteenth century that scientists emerged as a distinct professional community.

If pressed to provide a definition for contemporary science we might try: "Science is a body of organized knowledge that describes the properties and interactions of the material components of the universe." The "organized knowledge" part of the definition draws attention to the fact that scientific knowledge is not generated by a bunch of maverick individuals scattered round the world, but by an international community working within the parameters of strict criteria for what is acceptable as science. It also points to the way in which scientific advances build on the existing framework of scientific knowledge: the wheel is not re-invented at every stage. Indeed, the brilliant individual who pushes science into new realms does so in a manner that explains the existing knowledge base in a way that doesn't negate it, but rather is superior to existing explanations. The "material components" aspect of the definition reminds us that the scope of science is limited. There are many kinds of questions that science is ill-equipped to answer.

Of course, no single definition is sufficient to do justice to such a complex phenomenon, and although the borders between science and non-science may shift a little and be somewhat fuzzy, it is usually clear as to what counts as science and what does not.

This book is focused primarily on the interactions between science and Christianity, but irrespective of whether we ourselves have any religious faith, the impact of science on our daily lives is generally via technology. Technology involves the implementation of results from both the physical sciences, leading to faster computers, cell phones, microwave ovens and the like, and the biological sciences, making feasible the genetic modification of crops, non-invasive medical procedures and new drugs to combat disease. Scientific advances underpin technological innovation, but the driving force behind technological developments is often economic, political or military rather than curiosity-driven basic science.

Huge ethical and moral questions continue to face society in the use of technology. For example, is it or is it not right to ban some technology, such as nuclear power plants, simply because they carry enormous risks in the event of an accident? Technology always comes at a price, and can be divisive between those who can afford it and those who cannot. Should we continue, for instance, to pour more and more money into increasing the technological sophistication of medical care for relatively few people in the richer countries, when the same funds applied in "low-tech" ways to medical needs in poorer countries could have benefits for a far larger number of people? Does Christianity have anything distinctive to say about the use of finite resources on technology?

These days it is often possible, at huge cost, to keep people alive using modern medicines and medical appliances, long after the time when they would otherwise have died from natural causes. How do we balance concepts of the sanctity of life against respect for the dignity of individuals and the knowledge of the perspective of eternity in making decisions about keeping people alive on life-support machines? Such issues are ones where Christian faith brings particular insights to the debate.

Some characteristics of science

The aim of science is to establish *generalizations* about the behavior of the material world. Science is not so much interested in the particular football that was kicked to win the Super Bowl, but in such things as the general properties of the materials used in making footballs, or in the aerodynamic interactions that explain the flight of oval-shaped balls through the air. Science is not interested in the single stone that killed Goliath, but in the general properties of stones. Science generally ignores historical particularity but takes a special interest in reproducible events that provide an opportunity for the analysis of cause and effect. When "singularities" occur in science, unique events without precedent such as the Big Bang, then science tends to flounder in explaining their origins. Science is much better at tackling events that occur more than once, preferably in a reproducible manner, so that the causes of the events can be investigated.

Science depends heavily on *quantification* to establish its generalizations about the properties of the material world. Theories that can be established or tested within a mathematical framework are viewed favourably. Data are frequently processed using statistical methods to establish significance. Possible sources of bias are considered and quantified wherever feasible.

Science is best at addressing phenomena that can be *taken apart* and analyzed in their component parts in order to explain the phenomenon in question. This is the approach of the car mechanic—if you want to find out how the engine works, then take it apart. Such an approach is more formally called "methodological reductionism." Whether this approach can lead to other types of reductionism is a question we shall consider further in later sections.

Science is also good at answering questions that are answerable by *empirical investigation,* that is by investigation that depends on carrying out experiments. This does not mean that everything that counts as scientific knowledge is based directly on experimental results. Some disciplines, such as the study of quantum mechanics in theoretical physics, work with theoretical models that are far removed from the everyday world, and indeed may produce counter-intuitive predictions. Yet the veracity of the theories is based ultimately on whether they provide good and fruitful explanations of phenomena that we can observe, be those in a multimillion-pound particle accelerator or in our everyday lives. Other scientific disciplines, such as geology, are more historical in their perspective, reconstructing historical events from data collected many millions of years after the events. But geology, like other sciences, uses present-day experiments, analogues or theoretical models to deduce the conditions that would have given rise to particular types of rocks, or environmental conditions, in the past. As with other sciences, it is a fundamental tenet of geology that the way in which matter behaves is consistent and predictable: one particular

Scientific language is often very specialized

way in which this is often expressed in geological research is that "the present is the key to the past."

Scientific knowledge is often couched in a *highly specialized language,* which unfortunately may make it rather impenetrable to the non-specialist. But the language is used for good reasons, so that ideas can be expressed concisely and in a way that can be understood unambiguously by scientists anywhere in the world. Sometimes the language is couched in mathematical formulae. When the Royal Society was founded in the seventeenth century it soon made it one of its important goals to establish a scientific language that contributed to this process of scientific communication. Often terms are borrowed from everyday speech and used in science with quite different meanings, which can lead to much confusion unless their technical meaning is understood properly. Terms such as "black hole," "selfish gene," "protein denaturation," "altruistic" and so forth litter the scientific literature, but their true meanings cannot be guessed without understanding something of the scientific discipline and context in which they are used.

A final characteristic of science is that the theories or models of how the universe works, developed by scientists, are always *provisional,* in the sense that better explanations often lie just around the corner. Even such an influential and successful body of work as Newton's laws of motion was shown by Einstein to be based on conceptually incorrect ideas. The point is not that Newton's laws were wrong, because they still provide a perfectly adequate and effective description of how things work in circumstances relevant to many of our daily activities, such as driving cars or playing snooker, or even for getting a man to the moon. But in more extreme cases, such as explaining black holes, Einstein's general theory of relativity is required. The theories are simply descriptions of how the world behaves, and their utility is judged on the range of phenomena and circumstances over which they provide useful results and predictions. The so-called laws of nature do not control how things happen in the world. In the Christian worldview God controls the world. In this view the scientific "laws" and theories provide elegant descriptions of how God acts consistently in the world. Powerful they may be, in a descriptive and predictive sense. Often they are even beautiful in the eyes of the (scientific) beholder. Yet even the most successful scientific theories remain only incomplete descriptions of how things behave.

What is counted as scientific knowledge is guarded jealously by the scientific community itself, and the main gateway for acceptance into this body of knowledge is by publication in peer-reviewed journals. Can you imagine bank managers, accountants, lawyers or head teachers accepting that others in their profession should control what they publish? But that is in fact what scientists do—and their papers submitted to journals are not infrequently refereed by their direct competitors! Scientific prestige is even measured by "impact factors" which measure the number of times that a particular paper has been cited by other scientists when they write their own papers. Not infrequently a whole new field of study can be started by a single seminal paper. Arguably the now vast research field of molecular genetics began with the publication in the scientific journal *Nature* of James Watson and Francis Crick's two-page paper on the structure of DNA in 1953.[1]

One reason why the veracity of scientific knowledge is so carefully guarded by its practitioners is because their future work depends on its validity. Scientific research is constantly building on what has already been published. If that core of

DNA

A defining paper that changed
the history of biology:

J.D. Watson and F.H.C. Crick (1953)
A structure for Deoxyribose Nucleic Acid
Nature, vol. 71, pp. 737-738

shared information has a weak foundation, then the whole super-structure will be shaky and much time and effort may be lost in demonstrating the point and in establishing a firmer basis. This explains also why cases of scientific fraud are investigated and publicized with such dismay within the scientific community. As well as the moral deceit involved in cases of scientific fraud, there is also the loss of time, money and energy as other scientists attempt to repeat or to build on the fraudulent results, but without success.[2] Science is about truth-telling. If scientists were to stop telling the truth about their data, then the scientific enterprise would collapse.

Science is far from being a mere cataloguing of isolated facts, but requires creative panache and bold hypotheses to make progress. Scientific data are "theory laden," which means that they are often collected with the aim of developing or disproving a particular hypothesis. Scientists are passionate about their commitments to theories, a point well illustrated by the vigorous debates that occur at scientific conferences. The public perception of scientists as being rather cold fish in white coats, without any feelings or commitments is far from reality, as anyone who has spent any time in a research laboratory will know.

What does science exclude?

A problem from which some scientists suffer is that they become so enthusiastic about their science that they fall into the trap of claiming that scientific knowledge is the *only* valid type of human knowledge. This philosophy is known as *positivism*. As a formal school of philosophy, positivism is more or less dead, but the idea lives on in a popular version of the same idea known as "scientism."[3] The idea in scientism is that scientific descriptions of events are the only type of descriptions that really matter—all the rest is merely opinion. Such an idea is clearly not inherent in science itself but has been added on to science by those who wish to utilize the status of science for their own personal ideological purposes.

Demonstrating the weakness of scientism is quite easy. Take your favorite daily newspaper, read through all the news items, comment columns, latest film reviews and so forth, and then at the end ask yourself the question, "How does scientific knowledge contribute to an understanding of the particular items that I have just read?" The answer in most cases will be clear: "not a lot." Scientific knowledge is simply irrelevant to most daily human activities, which is what our newspapers are there to describe, but it is silly to pretend that these human activities are any the less important or interesting simply because science does not have much to say about them. There is an arrogance about scientism that is irritating to the non-scientist and is equally embarrassing to the scientific colleagues of those few (but vocal) scientists who insist on making scientistic claims in public.

More formally, what kinds of human knowledge are excluded from scientific investigation? Certainly aesthetics is excluded. No amount of scientific knowledge can confirm or deny the claim that someone is observing beauty in a sunset, in a range of mountain peaks, in a painting, or in a piece of poetry. You could of course plant electrodes in the head of the person as they had aesthetic experiences and made aesthetic judgments, but the data you would collect would not be the same as the aesthetic judgments themselves. And only a knave or a fool would claim that there was no reasonable basis for assessing creativity, because otherwise all reviewers of books, novels, films, ballet, the theater and so on would simply be wasting their time.

Scientific knowledge also excludes ethical and moral knowledge. Science can analyse the reasons for the latest famine in a particular country, but it cannot tell you whether you personally ought to give up your expensive summer holiday and volunteer to help the aid agencies as they distribute food. When people make ethical decisions they are appealing to forms of argument and knowledge that lie outside the purview of scientific journals. The "naturalistic fallacy" is the attempt to derive an "ought" from an "is"; that is, to try to derive judgments about what ought to be the case from descriptions of what is actually the case. Scientific descriptions are good at giving an account of what is the case, but they will never tell you what *ought* to be the case, which is what ethical decisions are all about.

Scientific knowledge also excludes all forms of personal knowledge and experience. If you submit to a scientific journal your description of an encounter with a famous scientist, the editor is unlikely to count it as a contribution to scientific knowledge (more likely it will go straight into the trash), even though the experience may have been life-changing for you personally to such an extent that it led you into a career in science. Likewise, if I am asked the question "Do you know John?," and if in fact I do know him, then I would be lying to deny it. But the kind of personal knowledge implied in that answer is of a different kind from scientific knowledge that I may obtain *about* John by measuring his blood pressure, putting electrodes in his brain or measuring the levels of certain chemicals in his urine. However important scientific assessments may be of human individuals in different contexts, they will never be the same as knowing-the-person. Knowing-the-person does not invalidate scientific knowledge in any way, nor is it contradictory to scientific knowledge—it is simply a different type of "knowing." For most people it is actually the kind of knowledge that makes life worth living.

Another whole sphere of human enquiry that science is poorly equipped to address is the domain of metaphysics. Metaphysics encompasses all the big philosophical questions of life, such as "Why am I here?," "Does life have a meaning?," "Is there a God?" and so on. Of course, those who hold to the philosophy of scientism will try to pretend that such questions are unanswerable precisely for the reason that they cannot be tackled by the methods of science and, therefore (they say), we can never find an answer. There are several problems with such a position. For a start, scientism itself is a metaphysical conviction that is beyond science, although parasitic upon it. It is perfectly possible to do good science without adopting the metaphysical position described by scientism. Furthermore, such a position smacks of intellectual laziness, since humans throughout history have continued to insist on asking metaphysical types of question, and just because science cannot answer them does not mean to say that they are unanswerable.

A somewhat different point was underlined by one of the twentieth century's great philosophers of science, Karl Popper, during a broadcast talk, when he insisted that:

> Everybody has some philosophy; you, and I, and everybody. Whether or not we know it, we all take a great number of things for granted. These uncritical assumptions are often of a philosophical character. Sometimes they are true; but more often these philosophies of ours are mistaken.[4]

All human beings are committed philosophers in the sense that they hold prior metaphysical assumptions that shape their actions and behavior in the world. So it is an exercise in academic arm-waving to suggest that there exists some non-metaphysically based high ground from which lofty (and mythical) vantage point one could then survey the metaphysical beliefs of lesser mortals. In practice everyone behaves within the framework provided by their metaphysical convictions, even though they may not be very good at articulating what those are. There is no such animal as an uncommitted human being. Those who hold to the metaphysics of scientism are already committed to living as if the great metaphysical questions of life had already been answered, despite their denial of such a possibility. Living as if life has no ultimate meaning implies a prior assumption that life in fact has no ultimate meaning, so the protestation that such metaphysical questions cannot be answered fails to convince. People are demonstrating that they believe such questions are answerable all the time by the way they live their lives, scientists no less than anyone else. Everyone has to live a life, everyone has to construct a personal biography, and this involves making a wide range of decisions on a daily basis that lie well beyond science, not least ethical decisions. Once we accept that we are all in the same boat and that no one in practice lives their life as if scientific knowledge was the only valid form of knowing, then the dialogue between science and faith can really begin.

CHAPTER 2

Knowledge—Scientific and Religious

There are some important similarities between scientific knowledge and religious knowledge which we will consider further below. But first let us consider the differences.

How does religious knowledge differ from scientific knowledge?

Religion asks questions about the same reality as science, but from a different angle. The old adage that science answers the "how" questions whereas religion answers the "why" questions has some merit to it, although the division is not always as neat as the adage implies. For example, science generates cosmological models to explain the current properties of the universe, whereas religion is more interested in asking *why* the universe came into being in the first place, possessing the properties that science describes. Science is good at explaining how biological diversity came into being by an evolutionary process. Religion wishes to address the ultimate question of *why* conscious human beings have come into being by this process, persons who not only can describe the universe in which they live but who also ask questions about their own meaning and role within it. Science is brilliant at describing the workings of the human body. Religion—at least the Christian religion—points out that human bodies have come into being for particular purposes, namely, to be able to know and respond to God.

Science and religion also differ in the types of information that they count as data. Scientific data, as already noted, are often derived from events that are reproducible, amenable to quantification, and frequently are accessible only by means of specialized instruments. In contrast some people would doubt whether the term "data" could even be applied to the types of information that are assessed when considering religious truth claims. It certainly has to be admitted that the types of evidence investigated in the scientific compared with the religious enterprise are usually different from each other, which is not surprising considering the distinctive questions being addressed in each case. Nevertheless, Christians would wish to point out that there are real data that anyone has to reckon with as they assess the truth claims of Christianity, as we will consider further below. And just because they happen to involve different types of evidence, in many cases, from scientific data does not imply that any less intellectual rigor is required in deciding between rival ideas.

A further difference between scientific and religious knowledge is that Christianity, for example, emphasizes the personal involvement of the individual in their commitment to God as they experience answers to prayer and God's guidance in their life. In contrast the scientist is asked to down-play their personal prejudices and involvement, as much as they are able, in favour of a more detached stance toward their investigation. In practice, as already noted, this is not so easy to achieve, but the distinction is an important one—more a question of emphasis, perhaps, than of a complete difference.

Another difference is that science is progressive, in the sense that scientific theories build on a previous body of knowledge, and therefore are always attempting to advance toward better descriptions of the natural world. It is for this reason that the body of scientific knowledge is constantly changing as theories come and go. The rate at which this happens varies greatly depending on the research field in question. For example, the research area of one of the authors (DA) within the field of immunology did not even exist 25 years ago, and the papers we wrote 10 years ago look extremely dated today. Science is currently moving on at a tremendous pace, especially in the biological arena. In contrast, the Christian faith claims to be a revelation of God's ultimate purposes for humankind that is eternal and unchanging. That faith is based on certain historical events which happened once and for all time—so there is no concept of "progressive revelation" in Christianity, as if we could know anything more about God now than did the writers of the New Testament nearly 2,000 years ago. Nevertheless our own understanding and experience of God's purposes can certainly deepen and grow as the Christian faith spreads to many different cultures, and as academic research helps us to understand and to interpret God's revelation in the Bible. Furthermore, there is a vast body of Christian literature—doctrinal, pastoral, missionary and biographical—which provides a body of

Christian wisdom and experience that is (hopefully) progressive in terms of building on the contributions of those Christian writers who have already contributed to this great corpus of religious knowledge in the past. Viewed from such a perspective, a body of religious literature does not seem all *that* different from a body of scientific literature after all.

Finally, there is a difference between science and religion in that scientific theories are often assessed by their ability to predict certain outcomes. If hypothesis A is correct then in circumstance B, result C should occur. If result C actually happens then hypothesis A is strengthened. Religious knowledge is not generally like that, although there may be some analogous parallels. For example, if the Holy Spirit is the life-changing force in people's lives that Christians claim (hypothesis A), then in the normal stresses and strains of everyday life (circumstance B), if 100 people become Christians at time zero, then after 5 years (let's say) there should be some definite evidence of selfishness being overcome in the lives of a good percentage of them (result C). If 100 Christians were all just as selfish as they were before time zero, then you might be justified in doubting the validity of hypothesis A!

What are the similarities between scientific and religious knowledge?

It is surprising how many non-Christians, and even some Christians, are under the impression that thinking about science and religion involves quite different ways of thinking, as if the two enterprises had to be kept in hermetically sealed boxes. Nothing could be further from the truth. It is a common experience of Christians who are involved in scientific research that their modes of discussion and argumentation are remarkably similar within both enterprises. Coming to faith is no blind leap in the dark, but a commitment based on a prior process of rational assessment and argument. Such similarities are most apparent when it is the "Big Theories" of science that are being considered, such as the Big Bang theory in cosmology or evolutionary theory in biology. The theory of evolution is a "Big Theory" in the sense that it links together disparate data from an extraordinarily wide range of disciplines—molecular biology, biochemistry, physiology, anatomy, zoology, botany, geology, anthropology and ecology, to name but a few—and makes coherent sense of this diverse body of observations. That is the reason why it is such a powerful theory, because it explains so much, so well. Non-biologists who are suspicious of the truth-claims of evolutionary theory are sometimes frustrated when they see anomalies in the theory, because biologists often appear so sanguine about the possibility of eventually resolving the anomalies. But this is always the characteristic of a successful Big Theory of science. The Theory is so successful in explaining so much that it can afford to brush off the odd anomaly in the expectation that it will be resolved by further research. Of course there is always the possibility that anomalies will continue to accumulate until they bring the theory crashing to the ground as a new and better theory is ushered in. But until that day comes, scientists will be content to operate within the paradigm of the Big Theory.

There are some remarkable similarities between the way scientists assess Big Theories in science, and the way in which Christian theism, for example, can be assessed as an inference to the best explanation for the existence of the kind of universe in which we live.[1] The framework provided by Christian theism suggests that there is a personal creator God who has willed this particular universe into being, having properties intended for the development of self-aware humans who will therefore have the possibility of making moral choices, and in particular of making the choice as to whether to enter into a relationship with God.

In terms of ultimate explanations for the existence of the properties of the universe we inhabit, Christian theism therefore provides an explanation that is both elegant and coherent in the sense that, like evolutionary theory in biology, it draws together many disparate types of data. As examples of such widely ranging data, Christians might choose to cite the extraordinary fine-tuning of the physical constants that make the existence of life possible, the existence of good and evil in the world, the experience of listening to, say, Bach's *St Matthew's Passion,* the exhilaration of standing on the peak of a mountain range, the depth of love experienced in a close relationship, personal experiences of answered prayer, the historical evidence for the resurrection of Jesus, or the recorded experiences of Christians who have come to know God through suffering. It can be argued that such data are more consistent with Christian theism than they are with alternative metaphysical theories such as atheism, which provides no grounds for the expectation that one or more universes should exist in which personal conscious and moral beings emerge.

It is not our intention at this stage to make such a defense of Christian theism—only to emphasize that the mode of argument used in assessing the Big Theories of metaphysics, such as Christian theism, is not dissimilar to that used by scientists when assessing the Big Theories of science. The style of argumentation is very similar to that used by lawyers—the weighing and assessing of evidence and counter-evidence, argument and counter-argument. If you spent any time in one of our own research laboratories, you might soon become convinced that you had stumbled into a law court rather than a research lab. The two places are not dissimilar (apart from the wigs and the salaries), in the vigor with which differing ideas are challenged and probed.

It is sometimes claimed that since religion is a "matter of faith," no amount of evidence will dissuade religious people from such faith. There is plenty of evidence that this view is mistaken. For example, people sometimes give up their faith, often after a period of considerable thought and reflection. In the case of historical religions such as Christianity it is also quite easy to think up scenarios in which counterevidence could be produced which would make faith untenable. The apostle Paul certainly put his own faith on the line when he wrote about the resurrection of Jesus to the new Christians in the church at Corinth, claiming that "If Christ has not been raised, your faith is futile; you are still in your sins."[2] Given that the body of Jesus, had it still been moldering in some grave after being stolen by the disciples, could in principle have been produced at the time Paul was writing this letter, it can easily be seen that Paul was laying his Gospel open to refutation. Such a possibility was clearly more acute for Paul, writing soon after the death and resurrection of Jesus, than it is for us now, some two thousand years later. Nevertheless, if tomorrow an ancient manuscript is discovered in Jerusalem purporting to be written by a disciple of Jesus and describing how he stole the body of Jesus, and giving exact instructions on how to find the tomb of Jesus, and if excavations then revealed a tomb containing a male skeleton in precisely the spot described, then at the least there would be a significant counter-argument to the evidence for the resurrection (such evidence, of course, is certainly lacking at the moment!). Therefore, there are data that could, in principle, be produced to refute the Christian faith, just as there are data that could be produced, in principle, to refute the Big Theories of science, such as Big Bang cosmology, and the theory of evolution. Refutation does not belong only to the domain of science.

Neither should it be thought that the search for religious truth need be a passionate quest in which objectivity is thrown to the wind. Far from it, a religious quest for truth can be carried out with as much logic and intellectual rigor as any scientific investigation. Evidence can be considered and weighed. Arguments and counter-arguments can be assessed. The historical integrity of biblical documents can be researched. The personal experiences of other Christians can be investigated. But at the end of the day there are commitments. The scientist needs to be committed to their theory sufficiently to write yet another grant application and to slog away for long hours in research to see whether or not their theory really is true. If it is, then they may publish their findings in a scientific journal and receive scientific accolades. The Christian has a commitment, too, but of course its implications are very different from the implications of being committed to a particular scientific theory. Getting a scientific theory wrong, the most you can lose is your reputation, but getting a religious commitment wrong, you can lose your own soul. There's the rub. But whereas total objectivity is impossible in any human quest for truth, both scientific and religious enterprises can achieve a reasonable level of objectivity.

Finally, both science and Christian faith share a "critical realist" stance toward knowledge. To understand what this means, it is first worth recalling the understanding of science that was commonplace a century ago. In the "realist" view of scientific knowledge, it was believed that science provided a completely objective view of the world which was independent of the prejudices of individual scientists. The task of the scientist was to make a large number of accurate experimental observations, and then to induce from such facts a general theory which, providing it was supported by a large body of consistent data, was viewed as an "immutable law of nature." Discovering a law, in this view, was like discovering a new continent. This "naive realist" view placed the authority of science firmly in the techniques involved in the method of enquiry itself. Subjective value-judgments were consigned to a realm outside of science, making science itself the realm of facts.

The past century has witnessed a gradual loss of confidence in such a naive realist view. Thomas Kuhn, for example, in his seminal work *The Structure of Scientific Revolutions,* published in 1962,[3] suggested that science develops by means of a succession of "paradigm-shifts." A paradigm comprises the framework of beliefs that are accepted in common by a community of research scientists. When anomalies accumulate within this framework, science gradually enters into a process of crisis that continues until the revolutionary creation of a new paradigm. In making such a paradigm choice, Kuhn claims, "there is no higher standard than the assent of the relevant community." No longer is there a particular set of methods that gives to scientific knowledge its special status. Instead the final scientific authority now lies in the hands of the scientific community itself, which decides between competing paradigms on grounds that go well beyond the mere application of rules.

Pressed to an extreme, such a view leads to a relativistic view of science which regards scientific knowledge as determined more by the prejudices and foibles of a scientific community than by the properties of the physical world under investigation. It is precisely that view which has been promoted by various postmodernist streams of thought over the past decade, trends that we discuss further in the next chapter. A really enthusiastic postmodernist will view scientific knowledge as yet another power game in which a particular human community tries to impose its system of thought on others. But there is no need to go that far. It is quite possible to recognize the important input made by scientists themselves as they think of new theories and then try to test them. But at the end of the day those theories will stand or fall according to the realities of the physical properties of the universe which determine what happens in particular experimental contexts. So theories are constantly being refined, destroyed or established, depending on how good they are at matching up to reality.

This rather more modest view of the role of science is known as "critical realism." This emphasizes the conviction that science provides solid information about the real world, but information that is shaped by the convictions of the scientific community and which is invariably incomplete. In the critical realist view, far from being immutable laws, good scientific theories provide a series of reliable maps that make the workings of the physical world intelligible and which have predictive powers enabling scientists to explore new territory. Although far from perfect, the maps are nevertheless congruent with the data derived from the physical world as presently understood; they are not mere social constructs, and a strong commitment to the current scientific map is therefore entirely appropriate.

The "critical realism" espoused by most scientists sits comfortably with a closely analogous form of critical realism adopted by most Christians. According to biblical theism there is a real world, which is not an illusion, having physical properties that are consistent and reproducible because they are dependent on God's continued activity in upholding them. This world can therefore be investigated by the methods of science. At the same time, however, there are "data" derived from human experience and observations that require a canvas much broader than scientific knowledge alone can provide. These "data," which are beyond the self-limited horizons of the scientific map, are just as much part of the real world as are the data about the physical world generated by the scientist in the laboratory. They include the saving acts of God in history and a whole host of features of human existence and awareness that are rendered more coherent by a theistic than by an atheistic worldview (moral sense, personal relationships, the arts, etc.). The Christian theist, however, is a *critical* realist who is acutely aware of the limitations of human reason and who realizes that understanding of the world is invariably filtered through all kinds of cultural and philosophical assumptions. Nevertheless, despite such caveats, our observations and experiences of the world, according to this view, are not merely social constructs, but provide data that enable us to evaluate rationally the truth claims of conflicting worldviews.

The beliefs of scientists about the physical world, however incomplete, are in the final analysis shaped by the structure of that world. Similarly the beliefs of Christians, also incomplete, are shaped by what God has said and done in history as described in the biblical record. In the final analysis both scientists and Christians respond to reality; they do not construct it.

Is science naturalistic?

Naturism is the practice of wandering around without any clothes on. Scientific naturalism is rather different and refers to all those philosophies that deny that there is any reality outside that which can be described by the natural sciences. Naturalism is therefore a brand of atheism with a particular emphasis on the supposed ability of science to answer all important questions. Used in this sense naturalism is a first cousin of scientism, the philosophy which claims that scientific explanations are the *only* ones that really matter. Naturalism is a rather broader term than scientism. Whereas it encompasses people who hold to crude scientism, like Richard Dawkins, it also describes people who have a somewhat more sophisticated understanding of the limitations of scientific knowledge, yet who exclude any notion of God acting in the world.[4]

There is nothing in science per se that supports the philosophy of naturalism. Like scientism, scientific naturalism is parasitic on science, but is not intrinsic to the scientific enterprise. In fact the situation is rather the opposite. As we will consider further in the next chapter, believers in a personal God who acts in the world are rather well represented within the scientific community, and their relative numbers seem to have been maintained at a remarkably steady level during the course of the last century. The concept of "conflict" between science and religion, though still popular in public perception, is a myth which has passed its sell-by date.

Scientific naturalism makes the mistake of thinking that because science is highly successful at explaining certain physical phenomena, therefore it must have the potential to explain absolutely everything. But this is a non sequitur, tacitly recognized by scientific journals that exclude a whole range of interesting topics from their pages. As already noted, science is of little use in tackling aesthetic, ethical or personal questions, let alone life's big metaphysical questions. As far as the existence of a God who acts in the world is concerned, science per se has nothing to say, although as we shall consider in Chapter 3, the data that science has revealed do appear to be an embarrassment to atheism.

Within the framework of Christian theism, all that exists is created by God and is actively sustained by God moment by moment. Thus all that science can do is to try to explain, using the best methods and models currently available, the actions of God in the universe. If God is the creator of all that is, then there is nothing that a scientist can describe that is not created by God. The universe represents a seamless cloth of God's creative activity. The degree to which contemporary science can or cannot explain well a particular aspect of God's creation is completely irrelevant to the question of God's actions in the created order. In fact the Bible has no concept of "nature," instead viewing everything that exists as part of the created order. The word "nature" in current usage has picked up certain overtones derived from Enlightenment thinking which make people using the word feel as if they are referring to something quasi-autonomous—and even Christians can begin to think of nature as something independent of God. But this is the exact opposite of the biblical doctrine of creation! The Bible talks only of the creator and of creation, which includes everything that exists, without exception. There is no "nature" in the sense of an independent entity existing without God's continual say-so.

Therefore there is nothing "naturalistic" about science for the Christian, who rather will see their scientific descriptions as leading to worship as they uncover more of God's handiwork. Of course there are some scientists who hold to the *philosophy* of naturalism, but this refers to their prior philosophical commitment, analogous to the way in which a Christian scientist's prior metaphysical commitment colors their whole attitude toward the scientific enterprise. Naturalism is not a philosophy that can be extracted from science itself. There are also naturalistic lawyers, accountants, factory workers, politicians, bus-drivers and economists. All in their various spheres will seek to carry out their jobs without recourse to a God who acts in the world. But Christians doing these jobs will do them in a way that is opposite to naturalism—seeking to glorify God in all that they do with their lives as part of their worship. There is nothing intrinsically naturalistic about law, accountancy, bus-driving, or whatever, and neither is there about science. It is the prior philosophical commitment of the person that can correctly be described as naturalistic or non-naturalistic.

Christians have sometimes muddied the waters by trying to distinguish between what they have termed "methodological naturalism" and "ontological naturalism." By "methodological naturalism" they intend to point out that scientific explanations utilize methods that only generate data about the natural world. For example, "God" and the "supernatural" are not used as explanations during scientific investigations because they do not belong to the same explanatory category as do the various components and characteristics of the natural order that science attempts to describe. The term "methodological naturalism" therefore draws attention to the deliberate attempt made by scientists to restrict their study to those aspects of the universe that can usefully be investigated by science. In contrast, "ontological naturalism" refers to the philosophical belief that the universe as described by science is all that exists and enshrines the belief that there is no God or other agent outside of the universe that science describes. It is therefore possible, some Christians argue, to practice good science as a "methodological naturalist" without holding the philosophy of "ontological naturalism."

Is this distinction valid? The "methodological" and "ontological" tags are certainly useful, but unfortunately they have become paired here with the wrong word—a better paired word would be "reductionism" as we discuss in Chapter 4. As far as the Christian is concerned, there really is no need to attach the word "naturalism" to anything that they do as they carry out a program of scientific research. For the Christian, as already noted, *all* scientific explanations are attempts to describe God's universe—there is nothing "naturalistic" about them at all, either "methodologically" or "ontologically." As far as the Christian is concerned, the word "naturalistic" is simply redundant as an accurate description of *anything* they do in life, because their *whole* life in all its aspects is a specific denial of naturalistic philosophy. God is acting in the created order to sustain it moment by moment, and God is also acting in the lives of Christians day by day. The problem with attaching a word with strongly atheistic philosophical connotations to the scientific enterprise is that the enterprise itself can then suffer "guilt by association." Since the word "naturalism" is redundant for Christians it is best simply to drop using it altogether in reference to their involvement in science.

As far as the practice of scientists to exclude God as an explanation in their scientific discourse is concerned, Christians active in the sciences with a firm belief in the creator God will be as committed to such a strategy as their non-Christian colleagues. The reason is simple. If God is utilized in scientific discourse as if God were just one further mechanism in the cause-effect chains that science investigates, then God would no longer be portrayed as the author of all that exists, but would rather be reduced to the level of a material mechanism. God in Christian theology is the author of all material and of all its interactions, without exception. Assigning God's actions to one corner of the material universe would be like invoking the actions of the author of a novel to "explain" one small aspect of Chapter 9 of their book. In reality, of course, Christians believe that God has written the whole "book of the universe" from cover to cover, and all that scientists can do is to describe its contents. There is nothing naturalistic about *that*.

What is the relationship between scientific and religious knowledge?

Three types of model are commonly presented as describing the relationship between scientific and religious knowledge, which we can subsume under the titles of *conflict, concordist* or *complementarity* models.

The *conflict* model, as its name indicates, suggests that science and faith are basically at loggerheads and that historically they have always been so. This model is generally the one adopted by the media, partly out of genuine ignorance and partly because conflict is thought to make for better TV. Radio can provide the opportunity for a more measured, thoughtful approach, but some producers in both TV and radio (but fortunately not all) tend to like nothing better than people representing diametrically opposing views shouting at each other across the studio floor. Prominent British atheists like Richard Dawkins and Peter Atkins and the prominent US atheist Daniel Dennet thrive on the conflict model and it is therefore no coincidence that they are sought after by the media. Harmony is not good for rating figures.

People pushing the conflict model usually claim that scientific knowledge is the *only* type of valid knowledge. They therefore perceive religious claims about phenomena to be rivals with respect to scientific descriptions of the same phenomena. They are frequently "naive reductionists," believing that once a scientific description has been made of an entity, then there is nothing left to say. Some of Richard Dawkins' statements provide notable examples of such naive reductionism. For example Dawkins has claimed that:

> We are machines built by DNA whose purpose is to make more copies of the same DNA. . . . Flowers are for the same thing as everything else in the living kingdoms, for spreading "copy-me" programmes about, written in DNA language. That is EXACTLY what we are for. We are machines for propagating DNA, and the propagation of DNA is a self-sustaining process. It is every living object's sole reason for living.[5]

Now, no self-respecting biochemist would wish to deny that one function of every living organism is to pass on its genes to succeeding generations. What marks out Dawkins' argument as an example of naive reductionism is his suggestion that passing on our genes is the only "real" reason for living. This is merely eccentric. The argument is explicit in trying to exclude the validity of any other levels of description of human beings.

There are several problems with the conflict model that will be illustrated during the course of this book. For a start the model fails as a way of historically relating scientific and religious knowledge. It is difficult to find any contemporary historian of science who takes the conflict model seriously. The real historical relationships between science and religion have been both more complex and more subtle.[6] The notion of "conflict" came to prominence in France during the course of the Enlightenment in the late eighteenth century. In England and the US the notion of a science-religion conflict was not popularized until the latter half of the nineteenth century. It has been argued persuasively that the idea of a conflict was fostered as a deliberate policy by the influential figure of T. H. Huxley and his friends in the X-Club.[7] They did so, in part, with the goal of winning for the newly professionalized scientific community the type of cultural prestige and financial privileges that were then the prerogative of the Anglican Church. However, as we discuss in this book, there are no intrinsic scientific or religious grounds for such a conflict, which grew primarily out of the social and political circumstances of the Victorian era.

Another problem with the conflict model is that scientific knowledge represents only a small "slice" in the overall "cake" of human knowledge. As we have already noted, if you tried to tackle most of the issues mentioned in your daily newspaper using scientific knowledge alone, then you would not get very far. The high proportion of people within the scientific community who believe in a personal God also undermines the idea that there is some intrinsic incompatibility between science and religious belief.

The *concordist model* takes a rather different tack in proposing various kinds of fusion between scientific and religious belief. Far from being in opposition, the various positions that can be subsumed under the concordist banner all suggest either that religious beliefs can to some degree be extracted from science or, conversely, that religious belief generates scientific knowledge. In the former category, the French Jesuit priest and paleontologist Teilhard de Chardin proposed a grand religious evolutionary theory, inspired by biological evolution, in which the whole living world evolves toward an "omega point" which,

Teilhard de Chardin suggested, is the ultimate end-point of the evolutionary process. More recently, the American physicist Frank Tipler has claimed that the notion of eternal life in an evolving universe can be extracted from contemporary theories in physics and cosmology.[8] Another example of a concordist model is the creationist claim that biblical teaching provides a scientific account of how God brought biological diversity into being. Concordist accounts therefore tend to emphasize the various ways in which science contributes to specific religious beliefs or vice versa.

The *complementarity model* is one that has received considerable attention from philosophers of science and religion during the past few decades, and is the model most frequently utilized in this book to relate scientific and religious knowledge. As the name suggests, the model proposes that the same reality can be viewed from different angles depending on the questions being asked. Science describes phenomena with a particular emphasis on the question "how?": how does it work? how did it originate? Religious questions tend to cluster more under the question "why?": why are we here as conscious observers in this vast universe? why is there good and evil? why should we make ethical decisions one way rather than another?

The relationship between different colored maps of the same country commonly found at the beginning of geography atlases well illustrates the complementary approach to relating different types of knowledge. One map represents population distribution, another crops, another geology, another climate and so forth. Each map is valid within its own perspective, but all the maps together are required to do justice to the complexity of the geography and economy of a particular country. It would be silly to claim that one map was the *only* way of understanding the country in question.

The idea of complementarity is popular amongst scientists because it is intrinsic to their research enterprise. For example, the way in which different types of scientist investigate the workings of the human body generates different kinds of scientific information that can only be understood properly by reference to the language, concepts and instruments used in those particular branches of science: the biochemist generates chemical data about the metabolic pathways that enable cells to metabolize; the molecular biologist investigates the functions of the various genes; the cell biologist studies how cells interact together to make up organs; the physiologist how those organs coordinate the internal environment of the body; the neuroscientist how the nervous system organizes the body; the psychologist how the human individual thinks; the anthropologist how they function socially within a

What is a human?

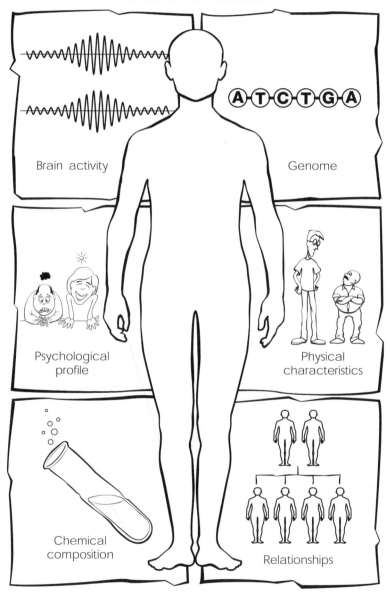

certain environment . . . and so on. It would be absurd for the biochemist, for example, to claim that the biochemical description was the *only* type of data that was of any consequence in understanding the human body. All the scientific accounts provide valid levels of description, which are complementary and not rival accounts.

The Christian would wish to point out that there is also a spiritual dimension to human identity that requires a further complementary level of description and discourse. This is the level that deals with the type of "why" questions listed above. The fact that historically no human culture has ever been found that lacks a religious belief system illustrates just how natural to human existence is this level of discourse. To the best of our knowledge, all human beings everywhere and at all times have been sufficiently curious to ask the ultimate questions of life. The naive reductionist may draw personal comfort by attempting to rule such questions out of court as unanswerable, but human beings insist on continuing to ask such questions. And so they should.

It must be emphasized that the notion of complementarity does not imply that there need be anything incomplete about any particular level of description. In practice, when trying to describe a biological organism there may be gaping holes in the completeness of our descriptions at whichever level we try to make them. But it is not this incompleteness which generates the need for complementarity. The need for a complementary understanding of the relationship between the various descriptive levels would be equally pressing even if our knowledge at all the levels were total. For example, if "all" we had in our hands was the complete biochemical description of an organism at the molecular level provided by a super-biochemist, we would nevertheless remain in great ignorance about that organism. Of necessity concepts such as "shape of nose," "how many legs," "reproductive habits" and so on would be missing from our description. The complementary descriptions provided by cell biologists, physiologists, anatomists, evolutionary biologists and so forth, would, in addition, still remain essential for a complete biological understanding of the organism. This would imply no slur on the work of the super-biochemist, but merely be a reflection of the complementary nature of different types of scientific information.

Many of the founding fathers of science had a strong faith in God and viewed their scientific work as a way of investigating God's creation. For example, Francis Bacon (1561–1626) made major philosophical contributions to the emergence of modern science in Great Britain, mainly by arguing effectively for new ways of investigating the physical world. It was Bacon who fostered the use of inductive reasoning together with the empirical, experimental method of data gathering. By so doing, he freed science from the constraints of metaphysical thought—the sort of thinking, for example, that considered a circle was a perfect figure, that God was perfect, and that therefore the heavenly bodies must move in circles. This sort of thinking constrained scientific investigation because it put theory before practice.

Bacon himself believed that the study of science led the mind to consider the divine creator, and thus to glorify God. He was firmly convinced that scripture was God's self-revelation, and wrote that scripture and nature were two complementary ways of revealing God's nature: "God's two books are . . . first the scriptures, revealing the will of God, and then the creatures expressing his power; whereof the latter is a key unto the former."[9] In this view of two books, the book of nature and the book of the Bible, Bacon was adopting a much earlier suggestion by Tertullian (160–225 C.E.), one of the Church Fathers who wrote that, "God must be first known from nature and afterwards recognized from doctrine; from nature by his works and from doctrine by his revealed words." This way of explaining God's dual revelation in scripture and in nature has remained a helpful perspective through to modern times, although for the Christian it is biblical revelation that provides the framework within which all other forms of knowledge should ultimately be assessed.

God's two books...

'Let no man... think or maintain, that a man can search too far or be too well studied in the book of God's word, or in the book of God's works.'
Francis Bacon (1561-1626)

God's word   **God's works**

In pointing out that complementarity provides a useful way of relating scientific and religious knowledge, it should not be thought that this implies that science and religion are locked in watertight compartments so that there is no interaction between the two.[10] In fact the opposite is the case, as is well illustrated by numerous aspects of the history of science.[11] It should not be forgotten that the "how" and "why" questions are about the *same reality.* The Christian understanding is that our faith should be a seamless part of our daily life—so there cannot be a sharp division between science and religion. What makes the religious and scientific answers distinctive is the type of question that is being asked. For example, a biochemist can ask scientific questions about the physical life of humans, which are best answered in the language of DNA and proteins. The same biochemist may also ask a quite different set of questions about human beings, concerning their spiritual life and ultimate meaning and destiny, questions best answered by the use of concepts such as sin and salvation. Physical and spiritual life are not rival concepts, but are complementary ways of looking at two aspects of human existence.

We will return later (in Chapter 4) to a fuller discussion of science and Christianity, and to the view that all truth is God's truth, so they cannot ultimately be in conflict. But before we leave the topic of scientific and religious knowledge here, it is worth commenting that there are many working scientists who believe that there is no conflict between science and religion.

To give just a few examples, a recent booklet gives the personal accounts of ten international scientists who not only believe in a creator God, but who believe that, far from denting their faith, their own research activities have strengthened their faith.[12] A similar, but longer book edited by Professor R. J. Berry,[13] comprising chapters by fourteen leading scientists who are Christians, gives a fascinating variety of insights into the way that their science relates to their faith. As the editor wrote, some described their intellectual pilgrimage and the implications of their science for belief; others wrote of their sickness, indecisions and disappointments. But all were explicit that they were where they were because of God's guidance in their lives. The common factor—perhaps the *only* common factor—was the certainty that the God of the Bible both cares and acts, and influences events and people for God's own divine purposes.

Finally, to take an academic survey of the religious views of scientists reported by the scientific journal *Nature* in 1997,[14] about 40 percent of the (North American) poll of scientists randomly picked from a list of names reported that they believed in a personal God and an afterlife.

This percentage was almost the same as that found by an earlier poll in 1916 by a noted psychologist called Leuba, who used the same questions to poll a random group of scientists from the US. In 1916 the results were thought astounding, as indicating widespread disbelief among these scientists; today the same percentage figures might still be thought astounding by some, as indicating a high level of belief among scientists.

So in practice there are plenty of Christians in the scientific community and most of them would see their science and their faith as reflecting complementary aspects of their daily lives and work. Complementarity is certainly not the only valid way of relating scientific and religious knowledge and is not a panacea for all circumstances. But the concept is a useful one.

CHAPTER 3

Is Science Discredited?

There is a crisis of confidence in science today that is particularly acute in the western world. It stems partly from over-confident predictions in the past that science was the answer to most of the world's problems—when the solutions weren't delivered by science, people became cynical about whether science was good for anything. Back in the nineteenth century there was almost unlimited optimism about the benefits that science would bring, a euphoric haze that was brought to a rude end by the technological horrors of the World Wars that followed.[1]

But you don't have to go far back in time to find bold predictions that now seem foolishly naive. In the 1950s, the advent of the nuclear generation of electricity was greeted with the pronouncement that electricity would become so cheap that it wouldn't even be worth metering it. Or on the agricultural front, the use of agricultural fertilizers, pesticides and specially bred strains of high-yield, resistant crops were forecast to make famine a thing of the past. Teilhard de Chardin captured this optimism when he wrote in 1938 that, as mankind evolved, "Disease and hunger will be conquered by science."[2] Yet as we are only too painfully aware, hunger is still an ever present reality for a huge proportion of the world's population. Teilhard de Chardin's optimism extended to his view that ultimately "evil on the earth . . . will be reduced to a minimum . . . hatred and internecine struggles will have disappeared," views which unfortunately do not seem to conform to the reality of our experience, or to the testimony of history. The Bible is clear that it is out of the hearts of people that evil comes (e.g., Matthew 15:19), and that "all have sinned and fall short of the glory of God" (Romans 3:23), so we should not be surprised that the sinful and evil ways of humankind do not seem to change much through history, except in the manner in which they are expressed.

On a different front, the fruits of science in the form of technology have often been viewed as dehumanizing, particularly when they are used in military contexts. Nuclear weapons appear to be insanity writ large on a global scale. Industrial activity scars the countryside and pollutes not only our own country, but that of our neighbours, too. And the first use of new technology so often seems to be for aggressive purposes: thus the first use of nuclear fission was in the bombs dropped on Hiroshima and Nagasaki in Japan, some time before it was used for the peaceful generation of electricity; within a few years of the invention of the first airplanes, they were in widespread use for bombing, years before being used for the commercial transport of passengers. It all seems a long way from the utopia once promised by science.

A gut response has often been an unthinking rejection of technology and, along with that, of the underlying science. Nuclear, chemical and biological warfare are ghastly to contemplate, yet only made possible by technology. The advent of large international conglomerates with financial profit as the major objective often leaves little room for sustainable growth or for working practices that are friendly toward the stability of families or local communities and environments.[3] One gets the impression that the much-flaunted environmental concerns of some multinational companies are really geared primarily toward greater sales or local acceptability of their other commercial practices, rather than genuine care for the environment. There are, we should acknowledge, some notable exceptions to such an attitude, and many companies are beginning to realize that environmental care makes economic sense. At governmental level, it is sadly the case that the most highly polluting countries, such as the US, with the greatest opportunities and financial resources to take significant measures to reduce their deleterious environmental impact, are often the most laggardly in doing so, again largely because such measures cost money and reduce profits.[4] We will return in Chapter 8 to a discussion of some of these global issues from a Christian perspective.

Yet the ironic caveat is that all of us, and particularly perhaps the younger generation, readily accept the fruits of science and technology. Life in the developed world, and increasingly in the rest of the world too, depends heavily on technology such as the television, the telephone and the microprocessor. So feelings toward technology remain ambiguous. Some people remain intrinsically suspicious toward technology, more so in Europe and Japan than in the US, while others are techno-junkies, welcoming every new fad with open arms. The US has more personal computers than the next 7 countries combined in the list of top computer-using countries and around 70 percent of the population now uses a cell phone, even though the adoption rate has been less than in some other countries. The resultant fad of text messaging is changing the culture. By mid-2004 text messages were being sent around the world at a rate of 500 billion messages per year. At an average cost of 10 cents per message, this generates revenues in excess of $50 billion for cell phone operators and represents close to 100 text messages per year for every person in the world. Yet such developments pall in significance compared with the impact of some of the big biomedical advances of the twentieth century. Perhaps, in retrospect, the greatest hallmark of the twentieth century was not the advent of Hitler or Stalin or even the demise of the Third Reich or the end of the Cold War, but the scientific discovery of antibiotics. That development alone has saved, and changed, countless millions of lives.

The threat to science is not so much a popular distaste for the negative aspects of technology—indeed it is a good sign that people are aware of, and care about, such deleterious effects—but that by and large the population is ignorant of what science is and of what it can do. If we do not understand one of the major forces affecting our lives, then that is a recipe for disaster, individually, socially and culturally. Furthermore, since there is such huge scope to do great evil as well as great good using the power of modern science and technology, it is important that to be good citizens we should understand, and be aware of developments in science. Should genetically modified food be accepted on the supermarket shelves? Is the reproductive cloning of humans dangerous? Is nuclear power too risky to contemplate? As citizens of democratic countries we need to understand and to involve ourselves in such debates. Otherwise, for sure, someone, somewhere will go ahead regardless. They may do so anyway, whatever the social or legal constraints. There is a particular onus on Christians, of all people, to be active in debating such issues because on the one hand they have the command of Jesus to "love your neighbour as you love yourself" (a mandate for action), whereas on the other hand they should have a realistic view of the fallenness of humanity and of the possibility for evil present in every person and in every society.

The public (mis-)understanding of science

If modern science is one of our greatest cultural achievements, it is also one of which most members of our society are largely ignorant. Only 20 percent of American adults have even a minimal understanding of the meaning of scientific study and can be considered scientifically literate. A series of surveys in the US since 1957 concerning the public understanding of science found that only half of US adults know that the Earth rotates around the Sun once each year, with 14 percent thinking that the Earth rotates round the sun once each day.[5] Less than half the adults understand that antibiotics do not kill viruses, despite the fact that antibiotics are one of the products of twentieth century science that most Americans encounter on a regular basis. Surprisingly, only 13 percent are able to provide a correct explanation of a molecule, although it is a term frequently used in journalistic discourse on television and in newspaper articles without additional explanation.

In the area of medical science, fewer than one third of American adults can identify DNA as a key to heredity. In the area of food biotechnology in which the US is a world leader, as many as 10 percent erroneously think that ordinary tomatoes do not contain genes. Only 14 percent of adults are able to describe the Internet as a worldwide network of computers that could communicate to each other, and almost half of US adults could not offer even a general description of the Internet.[6]

Yet this widespread ignorance of even basic scientific knowledge is, surprisingly, matched by an apparent broad self-professed interest amongst the population at large in medical, scientific and technological topics. When people were asked about their interests in newspaper stories, it transpired that new medical discoveries were by far the most popular, followed by new inventions and other discoveries in science and technology. Sports, new films and politics were close behind. But only a minority of those who said that they were very interested in science and technology also claimed that they were well informed. Many people clearly perceive there to be a large gap between themselves and the world of scientific knowledge; and judging by the survey results, they are correct. As already mentioned, ambivalence about the effects of science and technology is common.

Such widespread ignorance of basic scientific results cannot be good for society. Decisions on such topics as whether to allow genetically modified foods on to supermarket shelves, whether to build a new highway or a nuclear power plant, or whether to ban some kinds of research on humans or animals, affect all of us, and should as far as possible carry approval by the community at large. The decision-making process on technical issues is probably not helped by the preponderance of non-scientists in senior political, governmental and industrial jobs. From the Christian perspective, God's command to us to be good stewards of the world means that we should make every effort to understand the way the world is, to the best of our ability. Otherwise we cannot make informed decisions and can hardly be good or reliable stewards.

Perhaps one of the major stumbling blocks faced by non-scientists is that they often have a caricatured and inaccurate picture of what science is, and of how scientists do their work. At first sight this level of ignorance seems surprising. After all, when children are young they generally display an insatiable desire to understand their environment and to experiment with it. Every parent has fielded endless "why" and "how" questions from their small children. In many respects young children learn about their environment in exactly the same way as scientists. They are curious about it, and fascinated by particular things. They find out how things work by trying. And once they have touched a piece of burning wood, they extrapolate to new situations and are wary, for example, of touching anything else that looks as if it is burning.

But in one major respect children are different from scientists. All of science today is built upon a body of previous experience and knowledge. The average honors physics student today knows far more about mechanics than Newton ever did, yet Newton revolutionized the way we understand the mechanical motion of bodies.

One of the inevitable difficulties of science is that there is a huge body of knowledge that simply has to be understood. For example, on the first page of one of our daughter's Physics revision guide it says "This is the most basic stuff on electricity there is. I assume you realize that you'll never be able to learn anything else about electricity until you know this stuff—don't you?" The same book goes on to comment that "Very often, the only way to 'understand' something is to learn all the facts about it . . . When you've learned all these facts, you'll understand it" [sic].[7] Science is an intellectually demanding activity for the very reason that it is built on a large body of shared knowledge.

It is no good ignoring the previous body of knowledge if we wish to make progress in science. However bright and innovative our ideas might be, they have to explain the observed facts about the world at least as well as any previous explanations, or people will simply ignore our ideas; and rightly so. Science is hard, and it may well be this aspect that causes much of the population not to keep up with it.

There is also another aspect of science which takes it one step away from our normal way of dealing with the world. It is often counter-intuitive. Lewis Wolpert has captured this aspect in his book, *The Unnatural Nature of Science*.[8] For example, when you move away from thinking of the world as flat to considering it as spherical, one's natural reaction might be to ask why people on the other side don't fall off. It doesn't make sense. There is an explanation, of course. It is the force of gravity that keeps us on the surface of the earth, wherever we are. But that is several steps down the line. It is logical, once you know all the background, but not self-evident in the first place.

The notion of a spherical earth is easy enough to grasp, even though that carries some surprising results. Once you move to modern understandings of quantum mechanics and the like, science is even less intuitive. J. B. S. Haldane once commented that "my suspicion is that the Universe is not only queerer than we suppose, but queerer than we *can* suppose." It is one of the hallmarks of science that it attempts to explain reality as we find it, and not as we decide it ought to be from some particular philosophical stance.

A major aspect of the public misunderstanding of science is in the realm of how scientists develop new theories. The caricatured view is that a scientist does an experiment, records the data, and coldly and methodically deduces a theory that fits the data. Maybe in part this is because that is how many of us were taught to do experiments at school and to write them up in our exercise books—with the firm proviso at school, of course, that there was a "right" answer, so if we found the wrong speed of sound, for example, we had done the experiment incorrectly, or carelessly, and had to repeat it.

Real science is rarely like that. There is, of course, a huge amount of often tedious, occasionally pointless and sometimes dangerous data-collection to be done by experimentation. Often scientists go down blind alleys. But the real scientific breakthroughs often come about due to creative insights by individuals. Sometimes such people describe themselves as having been doing something quite unrelated when the idea came to them: sitting in a less than gripping movie in the case of François Jacob, who won a Nobel Prize for the idea he had about the role of molecules that bound themselves to DNA; dozing by the fireside in front of dancing flames dreaming of snakes biting their own tails when Kekulé thought up the structure of benzene rings; walking by the seaside after a long frustrating spell getting nowhere with an important mathematical problem when Poincaré finally saw the solution; even sitting on the lavatory late at night when Christopher Zeeman, another mathematician, finally sorted out a theorem that he'd been trying to prove for seven years; or just sitting in the bath (and it is not only Archimedes who has claimed flashes of insight in the bath—showers just don't seem to have the same efficacy!).[9]

Of course, ideas don't just come out of the blue: the individuals concerned had often been worrying away, in some cases for years, about some piece of data that didn't seem to fit. And as Pasteur famously commented, "Where observation is concerned, chance favors only the prepared mind." Furthermore, sometimes the new theories were based on partial, inadequate, and in some cases even incorrect data. Yet the nature of science is that others can test new ideas in the same or in new circumstances, and it is this process that leads to new theories being accepted or rejected by the scientific community.

Scientists are also human and subject to all the normal human strengths and failings. Pride, desire to be first, commitment, fortune—good or bad—and emotion all play their part in the doing of science. When the mathematician Andrew Wiles was recalling in a television documentary the occasion when he first solved Fermat's last theorem (which pertains to how numbers behave), he broke down and quite literally cried with emotion. Some may think it strange to become so emotionally involved in an obscure mathematical theorem that you cry tears of joy when it is solved, but that is the nature of the scientific enterprise, and a good thing too. It is far from being the cold, logical and unemotional activity of the popular view.

Relativism

One of the philosophical assumptions that underlies science is the conviction that some things are right whereas others are wrong. The structure of DNA happens to be best described by a double-helical model. DNA is not a triple-helix, neither will it be discovered one day that it is a triple-helix. The triple-helical model for DNA is wrong. Furthermore, DNA is a double-helix everywhere in the world and for all people, irrespective of their race, geography, culture or religion.

Such reflections highlight the extent to which the scientific community operates with an understanding of knowledge which is very distant from the idea that all types of knowledge are relative, that is, that something may be right for you but wrong for me. While relativistic theories of knowledge have been popular now for some decades, particularly in the domain of ethics and morality, a more fundamental assault on the idea of "objective truth" has been given prominence by the rise of postmodernism.

Defining postmodernism is like trying to get hold of a slippery bar of soap when you are in the shower. The term certainly incorporates many different ideas, some of them quite compatible with Christian ways of thinking. Often scientists never encounter postmodernism in the course of their academic studies, in contrast to those studying the humanities, but ironically are exposed to postmodern ideas every day through their immersion in popular culture. Frequently they have no idea how such exposure is influencing the way they think. Scientists can end up believing in concepts of truth and non-truth in the laboratory, but then in their daily lives maintain a relativistic stance toward other types of knowledge. Such a fragmented thought life is not healthy for anyone, but is particularly inappropriate for Christians who wish to bring every aspect of their lives under the Lordship of Christ.

Despite the complexity of various postmodern streams of thought, there is one particular subtext that forms a common element in the midst of the diversity. This is the idea that all forms of knowledge are rooted in a particular language, historical context and culture. In this view it is difficult to know whether a particular language mirrors reality since the criteria for its correct use are internal to a particular linguistic community. All claims to universal knowledge, shared in common by people everywhere in the world, are viewed with suspicion as masks for power relationships. There are, in this postmodern view, no "grand narratives" (or "metanarratives") that try to make sense of great swathes of human knowledge in isolation from language and culture. All knowledge is "constructed" in the sense that knowledge is a human product.

Postmodern streams of thought only make sense when contrasted with so-called "modernity." The "modernist programme" in this view was the attempt by a previous era to define rationality according to scientific criteria so that all cultures, philosophies and texts were judged by the extent to which they conformed (or not) to this overarching standard. Societies could then be classified as "primitive" according to this presumed "gold standard" of objectivity and rationality. The ethnocentric stance adopted by modernism empowered western capitalist governments to utilize the benefits of a scientific way of thinking to drive their own economies forward, but at the expense of exploiting the less industrially developed regions of the world.

The impact of postmodernism in the humanities can easily be observed by switching on your TV (most TV producers in Great Britain are arts graduates). Turn to the PBS channel and it is quite likely that eventually you will encounter a documentary describing a particular subgroup of people within a certain society who operate within their own particular set of norms. The norms may seem odd to the average viewer who does not share them, but that is deemed an advantage by the producer who wishes to draw attention to the distinctiveness of their lifestyle. Prostitutes in a big Brazilian city; body-piercers in Dallas; polygamy amongst Mormons in Utah; daily life in a rural village in China; wife-swappers in Southend-on-Sea—all are viewed dispassionately but sympathetically by the all-seeing camera that simply wants to describe the way people behave without making any value-judgments upon their disparate lifestyles. And there is something rather attractive about such an exercise. People are allowed to explain in their own words and by their own actions the reasons for why they do what they do. The approach is a far cry from the older obtrusive documentary that overtly ridiculed the particular cranky human community on the other side of the lens because it didn't fit comfortably with the norms of the "grand narrative" provided by scientific rationality and modernity.

Christians, as well, may find themselves cropping up on occasion in the media, not necessarily in the religious slots, but as fair game for similar kinds of descriptive narratives. The producer has become the anthropologist, tracking down people who believe a bit differently (or, even better, very differently) from the people next door. Indeed, in the most radical brand of postmodernism, actual anthropologists present the worldview and recommended therapies of the witch doctor in Africa as being as valid as that of the white-coated scientist carrying out research and development in a large international pharmaceutical company.

The Christian critique of postmodernism should beware of throwing out the baby with the bath water. The Christian would certainly agree that the "modernist stance" was mistaken to the extent that it attempted to define rationality within the strait-jacket provided by science. This is the "scientism" that we have already criticized. In reality valid and well-justified human knowledge extends far beyond the boundaries of scientific discourse. The Christian would also welcome the notion that belief systems can only properly be understood within the contexts of their own particular history, language and culture. The very human role of the scientific community in constructing the body of scientific knowledge is also inescapable. It is of course flesh-and-blood people who speak a particular language and who live in a certain culture who actually do the research and who peer-review papers and thereby help to decide what acceptable scientific literature is.

But it is quite possible to accept all these valid points without buying into the central relativizing thesis of the postmodernist paradigm. For it is this thesis in particular that renders both science and Christianity untenable. Science, for example, rests on the fact that the universe displays certain physical properties that are coherent and reproducible. These properties can best be described by mathematics and physics, and the accurate description of these properties is the same irrespective of the language or culture of the investigator. DNA is not a double-helix in Great Britain, triple-stranded in Argentina and single-stranded in China. So in science there is a kind of "grand narrative" built into the fundamental physical properties of matter. These properties are the ultimate determinants of all scientific theories for, at the end of the day, it is the theories that have to conform to the properties of matter, not vice versa. Or, as the biologist J. B. S. Haldane once put it in more colorful language: "The tragedy of science is a beautiful theory slain by an ugly fact."

So the practice of science and the relativistic stance proposed by postmodernism are incompatible. The dominance of postmodernist patterns of thought in popular culture may contribute to the public suspicion of science that is often found in the western countries. There is currently a powerful lack of trust in the institutions of western societies, in particular those that embody any claims to authority. Big science, rightly or wrongly, is seen as being aligned with Government and to represent people in white coats telling the public what to believe. Scientists say they have found the "truth" but sometimes they can be spectacularly wrong, although to be fair to the scientists, Government has a habit of putting pressure on them for quick and 100 percent guaranteed answers when in reality the situation might need a lot more research—and even then the outcome can never be 100 percent guaranteed. But the general point remains that people who say that one thing is true and something else is untrue do not readily gain a hearing in today's society. But as a matter of fact this is what scientists aim at all the time. It is their job.

It is likewise the job of Christians to point to the central truths of the Christian faith: that there is one creator God of the whole universe, that there is one redeemer, Jesus Christ, and that Jesus represents the only way to a restored relationship with God the Father. The historical rootedness of the Christian faith goes a long way to explaining why there are such positive resonances between science and Christianity. The Christian faith depends upon the salvation history of the people of Israel that led to the coming of the messiah and to his life, death, resurrection and ascension for us. Our own salvation is based absolutely on these facts of history. As the apostle Paul put the point succinctly, "If Christ has not been raised, our preaching is useless and so is your faith."[10] So both science and Christianity depend on data, historical evidence that can be sifted and assessed. And if the data are reliable then certain consequences follow: some things will be believed and others disbelieved. Some claims are true, whereas others are false.

As it happens, the claim of the relativist that "X is only true for me (or for my community)" does not stand up to close scrutiny. For when someone claims that something is true, the assumption is made that we should also believe it. It would make no sense for the prime minister to say in a broadcast speech that "I believe X is the case but you shouldn't believe a word of it." Yet it is precisely this kind of nonsense that is involved in the assertion that truth is relative. As John Taylor has expressed it:

> If truth is really "truth for me/truth for my community," then when I assert that a proposition is true, my assertion need not be taken as a proposal for your assent, since you are a different individual and you may belong to a different community. But then of course, I have not really made an assertion. All that has happened is that I have effectively, in a roundabout, confused manner, expressed what I believe.[11]

So it turns out that when the relativist says that "something is true for me but not for you," what they are *really* saying is "I believe X in contrast to you who believe Y." But in that case it would surely be clearer to talk about beliefs and not muddy the waters by talking about things that are "true for me." For once we understand that people are talking about their beliefs, we can then go on to ask the obvious question: "Yes, but why do you believe what you do believe?"

The confusion between truth and belief can readily be highlighted by the person who responds to the relativist: "Yes, well, relativism may be true for you but it's not true for me." If the relativist agrees, then clearly they cannot be making an assertion about truth that expects our assent. But if they disagree, then it sounds as if they are defending an absolute, which casts doubt on their assertion that truth is private to them or to their community.

The conceptual confusion arises from the relativist's failure to distinguish carefully between the assertion that a proposition is true and expressions of personal belief or opinion. For genuine communication to occur, it must be the case that truth is more than simply opinion. Imagine a world in which all assertions are no more than personal opinions. The chemist proposes a dosage of 30 pills a day as a good idea to start with, rather than 3 a day as the doctor prescribed. Your daughter suggests that your car would run much better on diesel. The referee asserts that Liverpool played so well that they deserved the third goal that knocked Arsenal out of the cup, even though an action replay revealed that the ball never crossed the line. Never mind, if it's true for the ref, then it's a valid goal. . . .

In reality a world in which personal opinion rather than truth became the main arbiter for action would be a nightmare world in which we would never quite be sure what had happened, nor what might happen next. For in the real world truth-telling is so embedded in the warp and woof of daily life that we take it for granted. A world in which a clear distinction is made between truth and belief or personal opinion is conducive to both scientific and Christian thought. Christians should be alert, however, to the extent to which the relativism promoted by postmodernism has filtered into many areas of everyday life. It will often be necessary to call the bluff of the relativist and to enquire how they justify their beliefs. For if relativism ever becomes the dominant philosophy accepted by societies, then science certainly will be discredited.

A Christian view of science

What is so striking as we begin to introduce Christian attitudes toward science is the extent to which science and Christian faith are blood-brothers, sharing so much in common in their ways of thinking about knowledge, in their attitude toward objectivity and truth, and in their shared commitment to describing reality: "the way it is," not just the way we might like it to be.

The Christian view is that all matter is created by God and is therefore good, because God himself says that he is pleased with it.[12] The task of scientists is to attempt to describe the behavior of the material of which the universe is made. Such a scientific study can only ever provide a partial understanding of the universe and of our place in it. It can answer the question of how the materials of which the universe is made interact, but it can never answer the question of why the universe exists, or of why we are here in the first place. Such questions can only be answered by revelation from the creator of the universe himself, who exists independently of it. Christians believe that God provides that knowledge by means of the biblical revelation.

However good our scientific understanding of the universe, it cannot of itself either prove or disprove the existence of God, since it only deals with the interactions between matter. William Buckland, who was a geologist at the University of Oxford and also dean of Westminster, wrote as long ago as 1836 that "no one who believes the Bible to be the word of God has cause to fear any discrepancy between this, his word, and the results of any discoveries respecting the nature of his works."[13] Numerous scientists who are Christians have made the same point. For example, Bernard Ramm, writing about a Christian view of science and the Bible says that "if the author of nature and scripture are the same God, then the two books of God must eventually recite the same story." So we should "pay due respect to *both* science and scripture. Neither adoration of one nor bigoted condemnation of the other is correct."[14]

Science is a tool for understanding the way in which the world works. Like all tools, it can be used for good or for evil. There are undoubtedly things that, one day, may be scientifically feasible, such as the cloning of human beings, which Christians will want to place off-limits for overriding ethical or moral reasons.[15] Some research may have specific goals that Christians would believe it wrong to support. An example might be research to develop specific chemicals that could paralyze humans faster in chemical warfare. But in itself, scientific knowledge is neutral.

Over the years, scientific theories have been used to support a wide range of philosophical viewpoints. Darwinian ideas have been used to bolster a whole range of political stances, including some which are diametrically opposed, such as fascism and socialism. Sociologists have explored a wide range of fields where they believe that Darwinism has had an impact, extending through archaeology, linguistics, literature, music and even social movements like feminism. Prominent atheists have appealed for support from both biological and cosmological theories, while New Age thinkers such as Capra[16] have used similar scientific theories to expound the opposite view, a pantheistic view that god is everywhere and in everything in the world.

All such philosophical theories are doomed in their appeal to science. Of itself, science simply cannot bear this weight of philosophical baggage. And in any case, the inevitable changes in scientific understanding that happen with time mean that the foundations of the philosophical superstructures are liable to move underfoot as the scientific theories themselves change.

For the Christian, however, science can be a strong ally, not because of its specific theories but because of its overall stance toward human knowledge. The business of science is to describe the world around us, and it is predicated on a belief that there is an objective and fundamental reality to be described. To be sure, scientific theories and explanations are but approximations to that reality. As we learn more about the universe, our descriptions of it become fuller and approach that reality more closely. But the underpinning belief that there is an objective reality to be known cuts through the relativism of postmodernism and the mysticism of New Age thinking.

In other ways, too, the Christian has cause to be grateful to science. Improved scientific knowledge provides immense potential for serving mankind through the alleviation of suffering and the improvement of living conditions. The process of scientific research itself also has many commendable qualities that are sorely needed on this planet in the twenty-first century. Science is, and always has been, a uniquely co-operative and community enterprise, albeit occasionally fostering gifted individuals within its ranks who have provided new directions and leadership. Science is built on a common body of shared knowledge and understanding. It is one of the few human activities of our age which effectively cut across barriers of nationality, ethnicity, religion, culture, sex and age. As such, science may be a powerful force for unity and cooperation in an increasingly fragmented world. Christians, who are called to be peacemakers, should be grateful for that.

Last, there is a strong sense in which the study of God's creation can point us to the reality of the existence of the living, creator God. It is hardly surprising that this should be so: if we are God's creatures, living in his created world, then it is natural that we should find an affinity, a sense of being "at home" in this environment. Almost everyone probably experiences from time to time a sense of beauty, of awe, and of oneness with creation in the presence of a beautiful sunset, a grand vista, a tinkling stream, or perhaps a particular blossom on a plant. Many scientists have expressed similar feelings that have come about through their scientific work, as they have studied the way in which created matter behaves. Kepler captured these feelings in a prayer with which he concluded one of his works on astronomy,[17] and with which we shall end this chapter:

> I give thee thanks, O Lord and Creator, that thou hast gladdened me by thy creation, when I was enraptured by the work of thy hands. Behold, I have here completed a work of my calling, with as much of intellectual strength as thou hast granted me. I have declared the praise of thy works to the men who will read the evidences of it, so far as my finite spirit could comprehend them in their infinity. . . . Have I been seduced into presumption by the admirable beauty of thy works, or have I sought my own glory among men, in the construction of a work designed for thy honour? O then graciously and mercifully forgive me; and finally grant me this favour, that this work may never be injurious, but may conduce to thy glory and the good of souls.

CHAPTER 4

Is Religion Discredited?

The religious attitudes of individuals to science cover a huge spectrum: from full-blown atheism at one end of the spectrum to robust theism at the other, with undoubtedly a large group in the middle who never give it a second thought. A feature that many of these responses has in common is to hijack science in support of some particular philosophy, in the belief that a particular scientific theory—or even science itself—underpins the philosophical position being adopted.

In reality all scientists come to do science with their prior philosophical commitments already in place—they do not derive their religious or anti-religious philosophies from science itself. Since the business of scientists is to describe the material world to the best of their ability, the results of this purely descriptive and analytical enterprise may well provide evidence in support of, or against, some philosophical stance. But science can never of itself provide a philosophical basis for why the universe is here, what the purpose behind it may be, or indeed whether there is any purpose at all.

Whether consciously or not, everyone approaches their daily life with a set of presuppositions. For example, the Christian believes that God answers prayer and that events in his or her life are subject to God's providential control. A practical outworking of this is Paul the Apostle's comment that "we know that in all things God works for the good of those who love him."[1] But not everyone would necessarily see the same events in a person's life in the same light. Where the Christian may see God's hand in some set of circumstances, the unbeliever might write them off as "simply" chance or coincidence.

It is this aspect of Christian faith—to see God's sovereign plan in all events—that through the years has given believers in all kinds of situations, whether tragic, joyful, or simply mundane, an underlying peace and assurance that is inexplicable in normal human terms. Paul captured this aspect of the Christian experience when he wrote that he had "learned to be content whatever the circumstances . . . in any and every situation, whether well fed or hungry, whether living in plenty or in want."[2]

Just as these underlying approaches to life affect our daily practical and emotional responses to events, they also affect our attitude to science. The Christian believes that matter is good, because God has pronounced it so, and that to investigate it by the scientific method is a worthwhile and useful activity. Part, at least, of the reason we embrace a particular philosophical or religious approach is that it provides the best, the fullest and the most coherent explanation of the evidence before us—which we detect with our senses, probe with our intellect, and experience through our emotions. In other words we accept a particular approach because it makes sense of our lives. The results of scientific investigations form part of that panoply of evidence that has to be consistent with our philosophy if we are to live lives of integrity and consistency: our faith and our daily lives should be part of the same seamless tapestry of beliefs and practices.

The approach suggested in this book is that a robust theistic view of the world makes the best, most consistent sense of our experience of it, both from an investigation of its material properties, as provided by science, and from the perspective of Godrevelation found in the Bible. In the next chapter we expand more fully on a Christian response to science; in this chapter we briefly review some of the other philosophical stances that have been adopted when assessing the scope and significance of science.

Atheistic materialism

There is a common argument in circulation that because science is so good at explaining how things work, then ultimately, if we can come up with a "theory of everything" that codifies the interactions between matter on all scales of time and distance, there will be nothing else to learn. Then, as the physicist Stephen Hawking puts it in his best-selling book, *A Brief History of Time*,[3] we shall "know the mind of God." In the biological field, Richard Dawkins has become one of the best-known exponents of this reductionist viewpoint. He argues that because life itself is driven by impersonal and quantifiable forces acting on genes, therefore we need look no further for explanations of why organisms are as they are, or of why life exists.[4] Dawkins believes that organisms serve genes, rather than the other way around. Thus he argues, as we noted in Chapter 2, that the propagation of the chemical known as DNA, which carries the genetic information, is every living object's sole reason for existence—nothing more and nothing less. It is an arid view of life. In Dawkins' worldview, the theory of Darwinian evolution makes it possible to be "an intellectually fulfilled atheist."[5]

In themselves, such arguments have a seductive attraction. For one thing, they appeal to the side of our human nature that avoids responsibility for our actions—that likes to think we can do as we please for our own satisfaction. If genes are all the meaning there is to life, if what we are is controlled solely by our genes, well then, why shouldn't we do as our own selfish nature desires?

As science progresses, we do indeed learn more and more of how things work. The nature of science is that explanations of the observations gradually get better, often by small improvements, occasionally by the larger kinds of shifts in thinking ("paradigm-shifts") that we considered in Chapter 2. However, the simple step that is unwarranted, but which often slips in almost unnoticed in discussions with the atheistic materialist, is to move from saying that because we can understand *how* things work, then we can go on to make value judgments about whether or not they have ultimate meaning or purpose. To deduce atheism from the success of scientific explanations, as Dawkins does, is a non sequitur. It is akin to suggesting that a complete explanation of, say, one of Vincent van Gogh's striking paintings of sunflowers is provided by an exhaustive physical description of its properties: the various pigments in the paints, their spectroscopic response and molecular properties, the location, size and thickness of the brush strokes, the materials in the canvas and the frame, and so on. But, however complete the description, it would convey nothing of the beauty of the painting nor of its impact on the viewer nor, for that matter, the reason why van Gogh painted the flowers in the first place.

The success of scientific explanations cannot be used either to prove or to disprove the existence of God. To attempt to do so is simply to confuse the categories of explanation. Science only deals with material categories of explanation, and of the way in which matter interacts and behaves in the universe. Since it has that fundamental limitation, it can never address questions of purpose in the universe.

The strongly reductionist way of thinking that maintains that everything can be explained by the properties of its constituent matter has been called, in a memorable phrase coined by the late neuroscientist Donald MacKay, "nothing buttery."[6] To most people, the notion that we are "nothing but" a collection of molecules just doesn't carry any conviction. It doesn't ring true to our everyday experience of life, our sense that people are special and important in ways that are more than just the sum of their chemical and physical components. Least of all does it ring true when we experience the joy and satisfaction of deep human relationships.

But note that we are not saying that reductionism in itself is inappropriate: the methodology of reductionism is an important and proper part of science. We understand the complex world about us by breaking it down into component parts which are themselves easier to understand. Reductionism in this sense is a powerful tool of the scientific method.

But it is a big step from saying that the methodology of reductionism helps us to understand the way in which the material world behaves, to saying that the material world is *all* there is. This view allows no complementarity of approach, no possibility that there may be more than one equally valid way of describing what is happening. For example, if I see that the kettle is boiling and I ask my wife why, she could (though probably wouldn't) say that it is because there has been sufficient transfer of heat from the electricity flowing through the heating element to raise the temperature of the water to the point where there is a phase change from liquid to gas. That is a physical description of why it is boiling. Or she could say that she put the kettle on to make a cup of tea. That is a description of the purpose behind why it is boiling. Both are equally correct, equally valid answers. Both are true.

However good may be our theories of how the material world works, they can never tell us whether there is something more beyond the material. In particular, they cannot tell us whether there is a creator God who is responsible for the material world being here at all. We cannot infer whether God exists—or whether he doesn't—simply by studying the natural world. Atheistic materialism is an option that is not totally inconsistent with the results of science, but neither is it required by the success of science. It also has to be said that the fine-tuning of the physical constants of the universe, without which there would be no carbonaceous observers such as ourselves to do science, does represent an embarrassment to atheism. Atheists have no satisfying explanation for why the properties of the universe are exactly as they are in such a way that promotes the emergence of intelligent life. Or, as Stephen Hawking has expressed it so well: "What breathes fire into the equations?"

The Christian view is that God not only created the world, but that God also enabled us to understand something of those purposes in doing so, and of our place in it, by self-disclosure to us. To most people the hopelessness and aridity of a purposeless universe implied by atheistic materialism is one which, if they are honest, they cannot face, and one which does not satisfy their own (and Christians would say, God-given) sense of self-worth. Even Richard Dawkins, the high priest of atheistic materialism, was moved to comment in his televised Christmas lectures at the Royal Institution that "there's got to be more to it than that."[7]

The standard response of the atheist to such reflections is to assert that belief in God is a prop that provides comfort in an otherwise meaningless universe. But this begs the question. Whether something is a "comfort" or not has no bearing on the justification of a particular belief. The researcher in the laboratory may confirm, after a year of fruitless experiments, that their long-held hypothesis is actually valid. This is

The how and why of it...

a very comforting experience, as any scientist will know. It is a much more pleasurable experience than living through the months when the experiments don't work or don't yield the expected results. So it is quite common for things to be both true and comforting.

Conversely, someone who hears that their son has been taken prisoner of war during a battle might be comforted by the thought that at least he is alive. However, if in reality their son had been killed in the battle, their comfort would be based on a fallacious premise. So the question of whether a belief is comforting or not has no bearing on its truth-status.

Ultimately the main problem with atheistic materialism is that it provides no explanation for why the universe exists, particularly the finely tuned universe that we inhabit that has properties that allows the emergence of decision-making, thinking creatures such as humans who ponder the meaning of their existence. The speculative proposal (for which there is no evidence), that we inhabit a multiverse in which there is a large number of universes and it is just this one which happens to allow for the existence of conscious observers, does not lessen the genuine mystery of our existence one bit. For one is still left with the question: Why should there be such a strange entity as a multiverse in which conscious observers exist? Christians as well as scientists have this nasty habit of wanting to ask the question "Why?" and are not easily fobbed off by the answer, "Well, that's just the way it is." They want to go beyond that and ask: "*Why* does the universe exist?," or "*Why* do humans exist?" The answers to those questions take us well beyond any answers that science can provide.

The New Age movement

The New Age movement is not a structured organization, but rather a loose amalgamation of ideas that are expressed in a variety of ways and forms. It is probably the best general description for the views held by the majority of western people, albeit unthinkingly in many cases, since it encompasses aspects of pluralism, of relativism and of ill-defined spiritualism without making any hard-edged demands on individuals. It warrants our attention in this book not only because it has a broad popular appeal, but also because some prominent New Age writers have made claims that modern scientific results support their views. As we discuss below, we believe that these claims are unwarranted, and that science cannot be used to prop up New Age views.[8]

The New Age movement is, in part, a reaction against the spiritual aridity of the secularism that now dominates much of western culture. However, although Christians would say that a living Christian faith provides the answer to this spiritual barrenness, New Age thinking consciously rejects that. Instead, it proclaims a "smorgasbord of spiritual substitutes for Christianity, all heralding our unlimited potential to transform ourselves and the planet so that a New Age of peace, light and love will break forth."[9] The term "New Age" as a description for this loosely structured network of organizations and individuals comes from a common vision of a "new age" of peace and mass enlightenment—the "Age of Aquarius."[10] Christians, with their realistic view of the sinfulness of humankind, will view the idea of a coming new age of peace brought about solely by man's endeavours as little more than wishful thinking: others from non-Christian backgrounds might think it similarly implausible, though for more cynical or pragmatic reasons.

The roots of the New Age movement are spiritually in the religions of the East, although it has also been influenced by western secular humanism. New Age ideas flourished in the late 1980s after germinating in the counter-culture movements of the 1960s. New Age worldviews are characterized by anti-materialism, an exaltation of nature, a rejection of traditional morality and a fascination with the occult. In so far as it is possible to define the beliefs of those who identify with the New Age movement, they include four main ideas: *monism,* the belief that "all is one"; *pantheism,* the belief that "all is god," and that each individual is innately divine; *autonomy,* the view that individuals can do as they themselves please, since if they are god, then why shouldn't they?; and *relativism,* the view that since there is only one Essence, and since everything is part of that, then "everything that seems otherwise is a result of the way it is viewed, not its reality."[11] In particular there is no place for concepts of absolute good or evil, of truth or falsehood. Christian faith is inimical to each of these core beliefs of New Age thinking.

As far as its attitude to science is concerned, New Age thought holds in tension two opposite responses. On the one hand it is critical of the mechanistic, reductionist aspects of science, which it often portrays as being responsible for all the evils arising from modern technology; intuition and feeling are valued above rationality and the idea of objective truth that characterizes science. On the other hand it picks up some scientific concepts, such as quantum theory in physics and the Gaia hypothesis, and uses them in support of its metaphysical view of the universe. Some New Age writers have asserted that "we are approaching the end of science,"[12] as new forms of intellectual human endeavour will enable us to enter into "the higher dimensions of human experience." As

Ernest Lucas puts it, "this seems to imply that the scientific laboratory will be replaced by a seance laboratory."[13]

As an example, New Age writers often use ideas from quantum physics and relativity theory to claim that the material world, as we see it, is an illusion. They take the way in which Einstein related energy to matter in his famous equation relating energy and mass, $E = mc^2$, to mean that matter is only transient and that energy is the ultimate reality. Thus Fritjof Capra writes that one can "see all objects as processes in a universal flux and deny the existence of any material substance."[14] Zukav took quantum field theory from physics to claim that "interacting fields . . . intangible and insubstantial as they are, are the only real things in the universe."[15] Shirley MacLaine, another popular New Age figure, writes that "quantum physics was saying that what we perceive to be physical reality was actually our cognitive construction of it. Hence reality was only what each of us decided it was."[16]

All these claims make the mistake of extrapolating from physical models of an underlying reality into the realm of metaphysics. All that Einstein's equation actually says is that matter can be converted into energy, and vice versa, and quantum field theory simply gives alternative ways of explaining how matter behaves, that are valid and useful descriptions in particular circumstances. As Clifton and Regehr[17] comment, "it is treading on thin ice to attach a particular religious philosophy to the viability of often ephemeral physical theories." We would go further and say that you cannot derive metaphysical theories from purely physical descriptions of how the world behaves. There is little doubt that some metaphysical stances may be incompatible with the reality of how the physical world is, but equally certainly, many different metaphysical theories may be compatible with physical realities. We have already noted that materialistic atheism cannot be ruled out of court simply by looking at the material in the universe, and the same applies to New Age thinking.

The attempt by New Age thinkers to bolster their ideas with scientific theories is therefore problematic. Nor are these new ideas, despite the New Age name-tag: for example, they have much in common with first century Graeco-Roman Stoicism. New Age thinking is also incompatible with the biblical doctrine that the one creator God is distinct from the creation that God has willed into being. In the biblical view God is thoroughly involved with creation, which only continues to exist by God's continuing creative power, but God remains separate from the created order. Among other things, this means that Christians take the reality of evil seriously, and do not consider it mere illusion. In contrast, New Age thinking, like all pantheistic schools of thought, tends to blur the distinction between good and evil, because if "all is one" ("monism") then how can they be clearly distinguished?

Christians believe that because humans are made in the image of God, and the cosmos reflects something of God's nature,[18] then we can expect to have at least a limited understanding of the order in the universe that God created. Above all, Christians believe that there is a reality "out there" that can be studied and at least partially understood by science: this is in marked contrast to the relativism and inward-looking nature of New Age thinking. In practical daily living this Christian engagement with the real world provides a much surer foundation from which to face the trials and tribulations of everyday life than do the nebulous "feel-good" ideas of New Age prophets.

Natural theology

Natural theology became popular during the Middle Ages, but its roots are found not in Christianity but in much earlier Greek and Roman authors.[19] In fact the argument from design for the existence of God was devised by the ancient Stoics. Speaking for the Stoics, the Roman lawyer Cicero (106–43 B.C.E.) wrote that:

> When we see a mechanism such as a planetary model or a clock, do we doubt that it is the creation of a conscious intelligence? So how can we doubt that the world is the work of the divine intelligence? We may well believe that the world and everything in it has been created for the gods and for mankind.

The anti-religious objections of the atomists were also faithfully reported by Cicero:

> The world was made by a natural process, without any need of a creator. ... Atoms come together and are held by mutual attraction. Thus are created all the forms of nature which you imagine can only be created by some divine craftsman.

These two quotes from Cicero nicely represent the two major competing interpretations of the world that have been with us now for more than 2,000 years. Their contrasting perspectives are also highly relevant to our discussion of Christianity's "uneasy alliance" with natural theology, and indeed to the creation-evolution debate of more recent times.

At its most basic, natural theology can be defined as the attempt to argue for the existence of God from rational thought. With the emergence of modern science it was taken up enthusiastically by many Christian writers who followed the writings of the Stoics in arguing from the evidence for design in the world to the necessary existence of a designer. Although such arguments were originally couched within the framework of biblical revelation, as time went on there was a marked shift to give greater importance to the role of independent human reason.[20] This shift in thinking was associated with the greater role assigned to autonomous human reason that characterized the eighteenth-century Enlightenment. In some forms of natural theology, the over-riding belief became the claim that man could learn more about the world and about God by scientific endeavours than by listening to the biblical revelation.

Typical of this period, and immensely influential, was a book published by William Paley in 1802 called simply *Natural Theology*. It was to remain as a textbook of the subject for more than a century. Its central premise can be summed up by a simple but enduring analogy: if you were walking on the heath and came across a watch lying on the ground, which was clearly mechanically complex yet functional, then you would immediately infer that there must have been a watchmaker who had designed the watch. The argument is virtually identical to that used by the Stoics, as quoted above. The same argument was held to be true for the wonders revealed by science: they too showed, so natural theology maintained, that there must have been a designer God. Following Paley, a famous series of nine books was published called the *Bridgewater Treatises*. They were named after the benefactor, the eighth earl of Bridgewater (1756–1829), who paid posthumously for the first eight of them. Each of the books was written by a leading scientist of the day, and each described the "power, wisdom, and goodness of God, as manifested in the creation."

We should acknowledge, before we discuss why natural theology declined in favour, that there is nothing inherently incompatible between one type of natural theology and biblical theology. Indeed, there are several references in the Bible illustrating the way in which the created order was used to argue for the existence of an all-powerful being. Examples include Paul's claim made to the Greeks with whom he was arguing outside Athens that even they acknowledged that there must be a god outside the natural world,[21] and his subsequent proclamation that God's "eternal power and divine nature have been clearly seen, being understood from what has been made."[22] When writing to the Christians in Lycaonica, Paul reminded them that God "has not left himself without testimony" in the natural world.[23] The psalmist made the same point, that "The heavens declare the glory of God; the skies proclaim the work of his hands."[24]

But the Bible also makes clear that although the universe around us provides some solid grounds for believing in the existence of God, yet we need the revelation of God's character and purposes, which the Bible itself provides, if we are to have any hope of coming to know God personally. We could never have the faintest idea of the impact of sin on our relationship with our creator God, or of the redeeming death of Jesus on the cross, if we were restricted to studying nature alone. And in fact the great majority of biblical passages referring to God's actions in creation are written not to the unbeliever as an argument for the existence of God, but to people who already believed in God and needed to be reminded of God's care for the created order.

During the nineteenth and twentieth centuries, natural theology came under strong attack, particularly by secular thinkers (only some of whom were scientists), who argued that we cannot logically infer the existence of a creator for our own world, since we have no experience of the creation of any other worlds. Supporters of biblical theology also warned that the downgrading of revelation implicit in natural theology reduced Christianity to the arid ideas of "deism"—a universe set going by God but then left largely to its own devices—as we discuss in the next section.

As science grew stronger, and as more phenomena came to be explained by strictly scientific criteria, with no need of intervention by a designer God, scientists too added their voices to those claiming that natural theology was not required to explain most of what we found in the world about us. The growing self-confidence of science meant that, in principle, it was possible to explain everything in nature by a materialistic methodology. Thus, in conscious parody of Paley's watchmaker, Richard Dawkins gave the title of *The Blind Watchmaker* to his well-known book,[25] which claimed that there was no need to postulate any processes other than blind, random chance to explain the evolution of all living organisms.

Underlying these developments is a misconception about the relationship between God and the created order, a misconception easily encouraged by natural theology, which has been dubbed the "god-of-the-gaps." This style of argumentation depended on drawing attention to complex phenomena in the natural world, particularly in biology, and then arguing that God was the "explanation" for the existence of such phenomena. The argument appeared to be strongest when scientific knowledge was weakest. So "god" was invoked to "explain the gap" in our scientific knowledge—hence the term "god-of-the-gaps." A fuller critique of this approach will be provided below. For the moment it is worth reflecting on the obvious point that as the gaps in knowledge were closed—as they inevitably were—so the "god" proposed by natural theology shrank to smaller and smaller dimensions, rather like the fading smile on the Cheshire Cat in *Alice in Wonderland*. Clearly the "explanatory god" of this type of natural theology is not the one true God of biblical theology.

The legacy of the natural theology movement has been far-reaching. In our generation, many atheistic or agnostic scientists think that religion stands or falls on the viability of natural theology—and of course in most of their minds it has already fallen by the wayside. Since natural theology has been found wanting, then they are inclined to abandon religion, too. "What place, then, for a Creator?," wrote Hawking rhetorically.[26]

Ironically, natural theology began to make something of a comeback during the latter decades of the twentieth century. This occurred from two quite different directions. First, increasing knowledge of the physical constants of the universe impressed physicists and cosmologists by the way in which their exquisite fine-tuning has made possible the emergence of carbon-based intelligent creatures such as ourselves. Turn the dial a fraction on any one of dozens of physical constants and the universe would simply not have the properties necessary to allow life to emerge. Such "anthropic arguments" have led several well-known physicists to suggest that there must be some form of intelligence "behind" the universe, even though they may not believe in the Christian God. As John Polkinghorne comments: "When Fred Hoyle saw that carbon could be made in stellar interiors only because there was an enhancement (a resonance) at exactly the right energy to make it possible, he is said to have remarked that the universe was a 'put-up' job. Hoyle could not just believe this was a happy accident, with nothing more to be said about it."[27] Even though such anthropic arguments may not represent knock-down arguments for the existence of God, they certainly do play a role in encouraging people to think about the universe and its properties. As we have already commented above, at the least such arguments represent an embarrassment to atheism.[28]

The second type of argument for the revival of natural theology has come from a quite different direction, this time from the "Intelligent Design" movement in the US, which champions arguments not dissimilar from those found in Cicero and the Stoic writers, and which have cropped up in Christian apologetic writings over the centuries ever since. Since the Intelligent Design movement is a "first cousin" of the creationist movement, we will reserve a more detailed consideration of its merits and demerits to Chapter 6.

It will be clear from the discussion so far that "natural theology" includes a markedly heterogeneous collection of bed-fellows, and it is therefore wisest to assess each particular brand separately. Overall, natural theology is a sub-Christian response to science, not because it is wrong in all respects, but because it overemphasizes the importance of man's reason above God's revelation given in the Bible. It is certainly a right and proper response to stand in awe of God's creation, of its beauty yet utility, its unity yet diversity, its orderliness yet fruitfulness. But we cannot construct our understanding of God solely from nature. To do so risks viewing God as a remote, deistic figure rather than as the loving, concerned God who engages continuously with us and with human history.

The deistic response

Deism was a philosophy popularized in eighteenth-century Europe. In his *Dictionary of the English Language* published in 1755, Dr Samuel Johnson defined a deist as "a man who follows no particular religion, but only acknowledges the existence of God, without any other article of faith." The deists were convinced that they were defending true religion against the superstitious beliefs of the priests. The deistic philosophers attacked miracles not for their scientific impossibility but because they were "contrary to reason." Human rationalism was made the final arbiter of religious truth.

In the sense in which Johnson defined the term in his dictionary, deism remains the predominant religious belief of contemporary Europeans. In the intervening period the term deism has also come to be used to express one particular aspect of the beliefs of the eighteenth-century deists. This is the idea of a God who winds up the universe at the beginning, imparts to it certain quasi-autonomous laws which define its properties, and then keeps his distance thereafter, possibly occasionally intervening to carry out some special event. The eighteenth-century deists actually denied the possibility of miracles altogether as being "against reason," but deism in its contemporary sense is sometimes used to describe the belief that God is ordinarily absent from the daily workings of the universe, but occasionally acts to perform miracles. Such a deistic God may also be invoked to "explain" some phenomenon which science has as yet been unable to explain adequately. This understanding of God's actions in the world contributed to the "god-of-the-gaps" idea as already outlined.

The best way to understand deism is by contrasting it with theism. We have already introduced the central core beliefs of Christian theism in Chapter 1. Theism refers to the biblical teaching that God is intimately involved in *every* aspect of his creation, from its inception all the way through to its final demise. Many biblical passages could be cited to illustrate this basic doctrine, but perhaps the best way to get to the heart of it is by reading those chapters of Psalms, Isaiah and Job that express worship to God as the great author-creator of all that exists. For example, in the "Biologist's Psalm" (Psalm 104) we read that God, in the present tense, "makes grass grow for the cattle" (v. 14) and waters the trees (v. 16), while the "lions roar for their prey and seek their food from God" (v. 21). The psalm even tells us that when animals are born, God sends his Spirit and they are "created" (v. 30), using in Hebrew the word *bara*, the same word used in Genesis 1:1 to refer to the creation of the heavens and the earth. The present tense of God's active involvement in creation is also prominent in the book of Isaiah[29] where God says, "I form (*yasar*) the light and create (*bara*) darkness . . . I, the Lord, do all these things." In this and hundreds of other passages, the writers of both the Old and the New Testaments are insistent that God not only created everything at the beginning, but is also actively creating and sustaining this creation in all its detail moment by moment.

The language that the Bible chooses to use for God's continued actions in creation is not the language of providence (a word not used in the Bible in reference to creation), but the language of *action* and *causality*. Jesus said that his Father (in the present tense) "causes his sun to rise on the evil and the good, and sends rain on the righteous and the unrighteous,"[30] and this same God also feeds the "birds of the air"[31] and "clothes the grass of the field."[32] Talk of the "providence" of God can easily conjure up the idea of a benevolent but somewhat distant creator who keeps an eye on creation, but who doesn't get too involved. But the biblical language disallows such a picture. Paul wrote to the Colossian church that " . . . by him (Jesus) all things were created" and that "He (Jesus) is before all things, and in him all things hold together."[33] That is an amazing concept. Paul is claiming that not only through the power of Jesus was everything created at the beginning, but that now *in the present* the whole created order is continuing to exist by that same power. The writer to the Hebrews expresses the same thought when he writes that now, in the present, Jesus is "sustaining all things by his powerful word."[34] God spoke at the beginning to bring everything into being (Genesis 1) and goes on speaking to uphold all that exists.[35]

The problem with words is that they can easily become devalued by overuse or by misuse. Because the term "theism" has sometimes been weakened in this way, some people talk about "robust theism" when they wish to draw attention to this ongoing creative activity of God in his universe. Deistic thinking is only really shown up for what it is when contrasted with robust theism. Arguably it is impossible to be both a Christian and a thorough-going deist, because the "complete deist" will refuse to accept that God has acted in history to bring about our salvation through Christ. However, Christians often fall into the trap of semi-deistic thinking, frequently with the best of motives; the motive is often a perfectly correct desire to highlight God's creative activities, but to achieve this goal the semi-deist chooses to point to some aspect of the created world about which science is currently rather ignorant. For example, biochemical theories about the origin of life certainly remain rather sketchy and lack strong empirical support,[36] so some Christians highlight this current gap in our scientific understanding, but then make the unwarranted assertion that the origin of life can only be explained by the direct actions of God without the use of the secondary causes that science has the potential to describe. But this line of thinking brings us back once more to the classic "god-of-the-gaps," a line of argument that has five fatal weaknesses:

- From a Christian perspective, it fails to reflect a robust biblical theism. If God is brought into the argument to "explain" what science is (currently) unable to explain, then this strongly implies that God's actions are in some sense absent from those aspects of the created order that science *can* describe quite adequately. This point was put succinctly by Aubrey Moore, a fellow of St John's College, Oxford, more than a century ago, when he wrote with reference to such an "interventionist" view of God's creative actions that "a theory of occasional intervention implies as its correlative a theory of ordinary absence."[37] If God is the author of the whole created order, as the Bible teaches, then it makes no sense to suggest that the author "intervenes" in creation. You cannot intervene in your own novel. By invoking God's actions to "explain" gaps in our scientific ignorance you are therefore (unwittingly) undermining the biblical doctrine of creation. When the Bible illustrates God's actions in creation, it does so not by describing the spooky and the mysterious, but by drawing attention to all those normal aspects of everyday life in a rural society with which its readers would be familiar—rain, storms, wind, grass growing and so forth.

- It tends to reduce God to just one more mechanism in the chain of causal reasoning that characterizes scientific explanations. If God is there only to plug the gaps in our scientific understanding, then

God ceases to be the author of the whole created order, and becomes instead as if one of the characters in the novel. The Christian who therefore sets out, with the best of intentions, to draw attention to God's greatness in acting in particular aspects of creation, in fact ends up by belittling God.

- As mentioned above, the "god-of-the-gaps" will invariably shrink even further as our scientific knowledge advances and the role for the "interventionist" God becomes increasingly less (the "Cheshire Cat" syndrome).

- By introducing the concept of God to "explain" some particular physical phenomenon (such as the origin of life), it is often not realized that this type of explanation is in a different category from scientific explanations. Science describes the relationships between the material/energy components of the universe. Within a theistic framework, all science can do is to describe in human terms what God has done and is continuing to do by his use of secondary causes. Metaphysical explanations, such as those which invoke the concept of God, operate at a different level, and refer to the ultimate origins and purpose of the physical phenomena under investigation. The attempt to invoke "God" as an explanation for gaps in our scientific ignorance conflates two quite distinct types of explanation that we should be careful *not* to conflate.

- Last, but not least, the "god-of-the-gaps" argument encourages intellectual laziness. The Christian who is eager to understand God's world will keep going as long and as far as possible to understand his world in scientific terms. This is part of our worship. Some scientific problems may be insoluble at present with our current scientific knowledge and techniques, but the situation may soon change, and we should therefore be ready to meet the challenge and to throw our energies into understanding Godamazing world in greater depth. Gaps in our scientific knowledge are not arguments for God but reasons for doing better science. Christians have no hidden investments in ignorance.

The ostrich approach

Some people, even some Christians, respond to new scientific discoveries by burying their heads in the sand and just wishing that it

The ostrich approach

would all go away. From one perspective this response is understand-able—the rapid pace of scientific and technological change can easily outstrip the ability of individuals and of human societies to cope with the ethical and social implications of such changes. But in general the ostrich response to science is quite inappropriate. After all, if we are liv-ing in God's world, and if the role of scientists is to uncover more of the wonder of God's world, then Christians should be at the forefront of those seeking to push back the boundaries of scientific knowledge. Even if they have no direct involvement in the sciences, Christians at least should maintain some general interest in and knowledge of the latest scientific insights into the way God's world works. Not least it is important to do so because new legislation dealing with scientific or techno-logical advances, such as the acceptability or otherwise of genetically modified food on our supermarket shelves, depends ultimately on pub-lic opinion. However cynical we may be about the extent to which politi-cians listen to the public's voice, at the end of the day they are dependent on re-election at the ballot box, and they are influenced by strong public opinion. So as good citizens Christians should remain as informed as they are reasonably able, thereby becoming more effective in bringing Christian views to bear on topics of public importance. Many topical scientific and technological issues that are current today impinge deeply on proper Christian concerns, including stewardship of the environ-ment, protection of weaker members of society, and the biblical concern with the dignity and worth of every human individual.

Occasionally Christians are found jumping on the "anti-science" bandwagon. One reason for this may be as a reaction against atheists who try to utilize their science to prop up their atheistic ideologies. But we should be careful not to throw out the baby with the bath water. Just because an atheist tries to use the prestige of a particular scientific the-ory to support their own particular philosophy does not mean that the theory in question is wrong. Instead the false linkage (if that is indeed the case) between their science and their philosophy needs to be care-fully and clearly brought to light.

Another reason why Christians can become anti-science is be-cause they really do not want certain scientific truths to be the case, perhaps because they do not fit into their favorite theological schemes or some special interpretation of certain biblical texts. But we have to be careful to take on board what is actually the case and not merely what we would like to be the case. Describing the properties of God's created order accurately is a Christian duty. We should not try to live in Narnia[38] when God has called us to live on planet earth.

To take a specific example, it is difficult to avoid the impression that certain Christians are behaving like ostriches when they insist that the earth is only 10,000 years old. There are now numerous different dating methods, which together are effective at providing dating over periods ranging from thousands to millions to billions of years. Such methods show that the earth is of the order of 4,560 million years old. To deny these data, based on the intensive study of God's world, for the sake of preserving a particular interpretation of Genesis chapters 1 to 3, does seem to look remarkably like a head-burying-in-sand exercise. Apart from anything else, these ostrich attitudes bring the Gospel into disre-pute within the scientific community, since when they are publicized for their absurdity (as they often are) scientists then gain the impression that all Christians are obscurantists and believe along similar lines.

However, fortunately we are now finished with this rather negative survey of some sub-scientific and sub-Christian responses to science, and can instead turn to the more positive subject of how we *should* respond to science.

CHAPTER 5

Science Encounters Faith

Many people continue to think that science and faith just do not mix. If you have one, then you cannot really have the other, at least not in a rational way. If you have faith, then it means that you have to keep it in a separate compartment from your science. It's like playing golf, going to the leisure park or playing football—something you do on Sundays that's good for relaxation or your social life, or your sense of well-being, but not something that you would really want to relate to your working week.

Given such common views, it is quite a surprise to many people when they hear that there are plenty of Christians as well as people of other faiths within the scientific community. Not only that, but these Christians actually believe that there is a direct connection between their science and their faith. For a start, Christians and scientists share the same epistemological space. In other words, they have in common similar beliefs about what counts as knowledge. For example, they share the belief that some things are right and that other things are wrong. This sets them apart from the more relativistic theories of knowledge, as we considered in Chapter 3.

A prominent reason why many people, including Christians, are grateful for the scientific enterprise is that it is the fruits of science and the resultant technology that more than anything else can serve to ease the physical lot of humankind. You only have to think of the eradication of smallpox and, imminently, of leprosy from the world to be reminded of the enormous impact for good that can be made by the applications of science. And medical care, coupled with better nutrition and cleaner water supplies, has hugely increased the life expectancy and the living conditions of people, at least in the higher income parts of the world. Life in the pre-scientific world was not always nasty, brutish and short (although it was, often enough), but it was certainly a good deal less comfortable for most people than it is today. Ask people if they would prefer to have an operation without anesthetic, strapped down to prevent them struggling, or pain-free with anaesthetic, and you get the point.

As we discussed in the previous chapter, our philosophical pre-conceptions—the agendas that we bring with us as we look at the world around us—largely govern the way in which we interpret the findings of science. In this chapter we discuss how faith encounters science, illustrating this by mapping out how Christian thought, in particular, interacts with science.

The theistic approach

A theistic view of the universe means the belief that the one creator God made the universe for God's own purposes and continues to sustain it moment by moment. In this view, we can only know what God's purposes are if God chooses to tell us. And one basic point that the Judeo-Christian tradition asserts is that thousands of years ago God made it clear that humankind is pretty special, being made "in God's image."

What exactly does it mean for humankind to be made in God's image? The passage in Genesis chapter 1, verses 26–30, in which this is described, presents it firmly in the context of God giving delegated authority to humankind to care for creation. Rather than an intrinsic quality of humans, being made "in God's image" is more a statement of God's relational purposes for humans in putting them in charge of creation. God says that we are to rule over all the creation that has been made: the creatures in the sea, in the air, and on the land. Indeed, humankind is to rule over all the earth itself.

From the point of view of science, if we are made in God's image, then it is not surprising that we have the ability to understand the world about us, to care for it and to some extent to manipulate it. As has famously been attributed to the early astronomer Kepler, in doing science, we are but "thinking God's thoughts after him." Indeed, the belief that there is a benevolent and consistent God upholding all of nature makes it both possible and desirable for us to investigate the material world and to try to the best of our ability to understand how it works. This is in marked contrast to much of the ancient world, which was frightened to intervene in nature in case it caused the wrath of jealous gods, and which was inclined to accept fatalistically any natural calamities that befell it. It also stands in contrast to the New Age conviction that we shouldn't change anything in "nature."

In the theistic view the very consistency, comprehensibility and beauty of the created world are testament to God's character, and to God's care both for the natural world and for us. It would be a difficult, if not impossible, world in which to live if the physical laws were to change arbitrarily and inconsistently from time to time or from place to place. The anthropically fine-tuned constants of the universe are certainly consistent with what we know of God from the Bible, since the Bible makes it clear that God expressly created the universe with humans in mind as the pinnacle of all living things. We live in a universe in which God already knows "the end from the beginning."[1] It is that important element within the Judeo-Christian worldview which, most historians of science would agree, did much to nurture the emergence of modern science during the course of the sixteenth and seventeenth centuries.[2]

Matter is good

An important consequence of this robustly theistic view of the universe is that there is nothing intrinsically evil about matter. Given the fascination with material things of our contemporary society, this might seem like an odd point to emphasize. But in much ancient Greek thought, the material world was viewed as being somewhat second class compared with the world of spirit and ideals. So the "soul" was viewed like a bird in a cage, locked in the physical body, waiting to be released at death to fly away to freedom. This same stream of thought contributed to the more extreme practices of medieval monasticism, in which monks in solitary cells would undergo all kinds of privations in the hope that the "subduing of the body" would result in the "freeing of the spirit." Even today many people think that being "religious" has to do with denying the desires of the body and focusing more on "nonmaterial" things. It is therefore intriguing to read the very first page of the Bible and to note there that God declares (several times, in fact, so we don't miss the point!) that the matter he creates is "good" and that he is really pleased with it. Evil only comes into the picture when humans used that God-created matter for their own selfish ends.

If matter is intrinsically good because it is made by God, this then subverts the idea that by subduing our bodies we might reach some higher spiritual plane. Instead, the Christian view of human beings is a holistic one: it maintains that what we choose to categorize as a person's body, or soul, or spirit are indivisibly part of what makes that human into the particular person that they are. And God, as he showed through the ministry of Jesus on earth, is concerned with the salvation of the whole person. Therefore it is a right and proper use of our abilities and resources to use them in scientific study of ways to improve the lot of humans in the broadest sense, whether through medical care, through better provision of food or water, or through improved understanding of the outer reaches of the universe, the deepest parts of the oceans, or the inner core of the earth.

The intrinsic value of the material world means that a greater understanding of its properties represents an intrinsic good. Christians would go as far as to say that this represents part of their worship. God is honored as we discover more of how his remarkable universe has been brought into being and continues to function. An interesting contemporary illustration of that insight was provided recently by Francis Collins, while in charge of the Human Genome Project, the international effort coordinated from Washington that generated a complete sequence of all human genes. Collins was a vociferous atheist until his late 20s in the same kind of mold as the Oxford zoologist Richard Dawkins, but then he became a Christian. Writing about his own research work in the context of the Human Genome Project, Francis Collins comments:

> The work of a scientist involved in this project, particularly a scientist who has the joy of also being a Christian, is a work of discovery which can also be a form of worship. As a scientist, one of the most exhilarating experiences is to learn something . . . that no human has understood before. To have a chance to see the glory of creation, the intricacy of it, the beauty of it, is really an experience not to be matched. Scientists who do not have a personal faith in God also undoubtedly experience the exhilaration of discovery. But to have that joy of discovery, mixed together with the joy of worship, is truly a powerful moment for a Christian who is also a scientist.[3]

The scientist not only has the privilege of delving into the properties of "God's intrinsically good matter" from a theoretical perspective, but also of seeing new discoveries applied for the good of humankind. The physicist can develop a better machine for imaging cancerous breast growths, or a computer scientist write computer programs that display the output from such a machine in a more readily interpretable form, enabling doctors to make earlier diagnosis and treatments. Such examples could be multiplied a thousandfold to almost any area of scientific endeavor. A geologist's academic work on how molten rock moves through the crust might eventually assist in predicting eruptions and saving lives; a mathematician's abstruse theoretical work on number theory might lead to improved telecommunications that eventually help repair fractured relationships in a highly mobile and rootless society; or a biochemist's laboratory work on the function of some little-known gene might eventually lead to the development of new drugs to treat debilitating diseases.

Although the idea that science should find such applications is now a commonplace, it was not always so. In fact only in the nineteenth century did the applications of science really begin to make a positive impact on human societies, a process greatly accelerated during the course of the twentieth century. It was one of the seventeenth-century founders of the Royal Society, Francis Bacon, who in his *New Atlantis*[4] mapped out his vision for a society in which science would have real practical benefits for society. Bacon's vision stemmed from his Christian worldview in which mere speculation about the world, as practiced by the Greek philosophers, would be replaced by an attempt to find out "the true nature of all things, whereby God might have the more glory in the workmanship of them," while the practical application of knowledge was "for the comfort of men." So the conviction that matter is intrinsically good, because made by God, has had all kinds of spin-offs in the emergence of modern science and in its applications.

Today New Age and Green organizations campaign to prevent society in general, and scientists in particular, from "interfering with nature." Their concerns are readily understood—no one wishes to manipulate the natural world in such a way that it brings unforeseen disastrous consequences. Such possibilities require careful assessment and consideration. Nevertheless, it is intriguing that the ancient Greek philosophical thought about matter that tends to underlie New Age thinking pulls in a very different direction from the thinking derived from the Bible. In the Christian worldview it is a duty to understand and to utilize the good material world that God has made for the benefit of others. But the suspicion of engaging the world of matter that characterizes some New Age philosophies does not encourage such a stance. Of course there are proper limits to research, some of which we explore later, and we should use all care and diligence in trying to foresee and to prevent any unwanted side effects of the introduction of new technology: no one wants to see another thalidomide tragedy, which led to the birth of an estimated 10,000–20,000 physically deformed babies. But provided there are appropriate safeguards to reduce the risk of such disasters, the Christian view must be that it is good, for example, to experiment with new forms of genetically modified foods if they can therefore extend the range of crops, or make them more pest-resistant, and so lift the terrible tragedy of starvation; or of new drugs that might alleviate the pain of "natural" diseases.

Science in a theistic universe

Christians feel "at home" in the universe because they believe it is a universe created and sustained by God with particular intentions and purposes for humankind. This idea of a "theistic universe" is remarkably congenial for the practice of science.

For example, within a theistic framework it is not surprising to find the properties of matter displaying coherence, that essential quality without which all scientific theorizing would be a waste of time. The ability to describe complex properties of matter by elegant mathematical equations is a reflection of the deep underlying order in the properties of matter. All scientists try to assemble their observations and data into theories that operate like maps of increasing sophistication that make sense of what has been observed. The more extensive the map in its explanatory power, the more powerful the theory becomes. None of this would make any sense unless all the properties of the universe were linked by a network of mathematical principles. Christians see the outworking of God's creative processes reflected daily in their research work as they uncover more and more of the underlying coherence in the properties of the universe.

A theistic framework for the universe also means that the reproducibility of the properties of matter is expected. We take this reproducibility so much for granted that we forget that it might have been otherwise. The properties of matter might have been arbitrary or random. If they had been, of course, then we would not have been here to observe the fact, but Christians see God's faithfulness displayed in such things as the fact that scientists can carry out an experiment multiple times and, if they did it well, get the same answer each time.

Christians are also not surprised to see personhood emerging in the universe, because God is a personal God. For the atheist, the fact of our own existence is a puzzling biological phenomenon that could so easily not have happened. But the Christian sees God's intentions and purposes being worked out through the evolutionary process that brought us into being. The fact that we understand this process somewhat better than we did a century ago does nothing to lessen our awe at the way in which God's intentions have been brought to pass after billions of years of planetary history during which, truly, God has formed us "from the dust of the earth."

In a theistic universe, the beauty of the natural world also has an extra dimension. Of course anyone can observe the beauty of the world around them, or of the night sky, irrespective of their beliefs. But those who accept the reality of the creator God will see this beauty through a special kind of lens, a lens that focuses on the actions of an all-powerful God behind the majesty of the crashing waves, the cries of the sea gulls circling overhead and the vastness of the ocean beyond. As George Herbert put it in "The Temple":

A man that looks on glass
On it may stay his eye;
Or if he pleaseth, through it passe
And then the heav'n espie.

Can scientists believe the Bible?

The common idea, mentioned already, that believing in God means forsaking rational ways of thinking, is also often extended to discussions about the Bible. Doesn't the Bible contradict modern science? In the light of our scientific understanding of the world, how should we interpret evidence from the Bible?

It is worth remembering that the Bible is a multi-author work written over a period of more than a thousand years in different languages and using a wide range of literary genres. This last point is of particular importance: we find in the Bible poetry, prose, historical narrative, prophetic writings, parables and many other literary styles. Unless we take some trouble to determine the kind of literature that we are reading, as well as something about the historical and cultural background of the text, then we may very likely misunderstand what we read.

It is rather odd that some people come to the Bible, a text completed nearly two thousand years ago, and expect to find scientific information within its pages. Scientific literature represents a relatively recent style of writing and did not really begin emerging until the seventeenth century when the first scientific societies were established in Europe and the first science journals established. The early Royal Society in Great Britain, for example, made a concerted effort in their proceedings to express scientific reports using a specialized style of language. Of course there was scientific writing before this time, but it was barely recognizable as that literary genre that today we refer to as "scientific literature." Today the development of scientific literature has continued to the point where specialists in different branches of science find it quite impossible to understand the papers of their colleagues.

Characteristics of contemporary scientific literature include:

- attention to a narrowly defined slice of the properties of matter;

- exclusion of the personal;

- precise and specialized meanings given to words;

- an emphasis on reports of empirical investigation;

- extensive citations to show how the science depends on and relates to the work of others;

- emphasis on quantification and statistical analysis;

- discussion that compares and contrasts the results with those found by other scientists.

Given this highly specialized nature of scientific literature, it is hardly surprising that we can quickly jump to wrong conclusions if we read another literary genre as if it represents science, when really it belongs to quite a different kind of literature altogether.

It is therefore quite inappropriate to read biblical narratives as if they were scientific texts for the simple reason that such literature did not even exist at the time they were written. It makes no sense to try to mold a scriptural narrative into a modern literary style that did not come into being until many centuries later.

As in our own everyday speech today, the Bible uses the language of appearances. For example, it talks about the sun "rising" and the sun "setting," just as we do. Such language no more implies a particular cosmology than does our own daily language. It is the language of convenience. So the Bible does not teach any particular cosmology and, unlike the early Greek philosophers, shows no particular interest in speculating about the structure of the universe per se. Least of all does it teach that the earth is flat! The writers of the Bible most likely knew that the earth was round, along with other ancient writers of their time, a point strongly hinted at in Isaiah 40:22 (God "sits enthroned above the circle of the earth"). The idea that people in earlier times, even in the medieval period in Europe, thought that the world was flat, did not start appearing until the nineteenth century, but there is no historical basis for it. Greek philosophers, such as Plato and Aristotle, were passionately committed to the earth's sphericity.

The main aim of the biblical writers is to give an account of how God has interacted with humanity over the centuries, in particular through the history of the people of Israel, and then later through the life, death and resurrection of Jesus of Nazareth. This is followed by an account of how the first churches were established, together with a collection of letters written to those early churches. The Bible focuses on the working out of God's purposes in history, and of the response of individuals and of nations to him—a focus quite different in its aim from scientific literature.

The early scientists in the sixteenth and seventeenth centuries were fond of speaking of "God's two books," meaning his "book of nature" and his "book of scripture," and emphasized that we needed to study both to gain a rounded picture of God's creation. There are also, of course, times when our limited understanding may lead to apparent paradoxes which we ourselves do not have the ability to resolve. Scientists themselves are well used to holding sometimes apparently contradictory theories or observations in tension—more often indeed than the general public may realize. For example, sometimes it is helpful to think in terms of a wave theory for the behavior of light; in other circumstances it is better to treat light as particles. And sometimes there are observations that simply don't fit any of the extant theories: this doesn't necessarily cause the theories to be abandoned, because they may do a good job of explaining a whole host of other phenomena.[5] But the history of science shows again and again the limits of our understanding, and the provisional nature of almost all scientific theories. At the very least, this should make us pause before proclaiming that something is impossible or before assuming that there is an irreconcilable conflict between something we read in the Bible and some current scientific theory.

Nevertheless, the Bible narrative is firmly rooted in real places and real times; God interacts with real people, and in real events that were observed and written down. The Bible is not a theoretical textbook or a mythical construct. Writers such as Luke, the author of the Gospel of Luke and of the book of Acts, were meticulous in recording accurately the historical details of first-century Palestine. This has been confirmed by numerous archaeological finds. There are also times when the biblical narrative reports some physical events that in principle might be amenable to scientific interpretation or comment. For example, the miraculous crossing of the Red Sea by the fleeing Israelites, and the subsequent rout and eventual drowning of the pursuing Egyptians as their chariots became bogged down, may well be described by the interplay of tides and winds holding away and then allowing back the water in that region. Indeed, the Bible narrative itself hints as much, in talking of a strong east wind blowing the water away so that the Israelites could cross.[6] But the important lesson that both the Old Testament (Exodus 14:30–15:21) and the New Testament (Acts 7:36) authors draw from this episode is that God was in charge, and purposefully caused this to happen: it was a miracle in the sense that God's timing was perfect.

But having drawn attention to God's ongoing activity in the "normal" physical order of this world, we also need to remember that there are some events that are truly outside any of our experiences, and which seem unlikely ever to be explained by any normal "scientific" reasons. For example, dead men do not come back to life. When Lazarus died, an event recorded in the New Testament,[7] his friends and neighbours knew full well that he was dead. They lived with and saw death at first hand, in a way that few westerners do nowadays. And when Jesus arrived some four days later, they begged him not to go into the tomb where Lazarus was laid. They knew that the stench of decaying flesh would be overpowering (John 11:39). But Jesus chose to raise Lazarus from the dead. Although we don't know all his motives in doing so, we are told that Jesus was deeply moved by the grief of Lazarus' sister Mary and her friends, and that he wept. But it is striking that when Jesus commanded the stone to be removed from the tomb and for Lazarus to come out, he made it clear that he was doing so publicly so that the people watching would know that it was through God's power that this miracle was performed:

> Then Jesus looked up and said, "Father I thank you that you have heard me. I knew that you always hear me, but I said this for the benefit of the people standing here, that they may believe that you sent me."

Equally the resurrection of Jesus from the dead is not something amenable to scientific investigation. Science is good at investigating repeatable events but many historical events are by the nature of the case unique. Science per se has no more to say about the resurrection of Jesus than it does about the battle of Hastings. The nature of purported historical events rests on a cumulative case where different kinds of evidence have to be weighed and assessed. As it happens, the historical evidence for the bodily resurrection of Jesus is remarkably strong and without that pivotal event the Christian movement would never have taken off as it did.

If Jesus was truly the Son of God as he claimed, then it would in fact be surprising if death could hold him in the grave. It would not make much sense if the creator and sustainer of life could be destroyed by death. If we knew that resurrections happened every Thursday regularly at 1:00 p.m., we could have all our instruments ready and undertake a proper investigation. But there is nothing that scientists as scientists can say about the matter. Nevertheless, the aftermath of such events caused indelible changes to the world that we are able to observe. The resurrection of Jesus certainly had an immense impact on countless millions of people, including several hundred who reported seeing him themselves in the immediately following weeks. The extent to which we are willing to consider the evidence for the resurrection of Jesus will of course be influenced by the extent to which we are willing to consider the existence of a creator God who upholds the universe.

The history of the relationship between science and faith provides some interesting (and sometimes depressing) examples of what can happen when people start reading the Bible as if it contains scientific literature. The historical example that immediately springs to mind is that of the conflict between Galileo and the Holy Office of the Inquisition of the Roman Catholic Church in the seventeenth century, over whether the earth goes round the sun or vice versa. One problem was that the cosmology of Aristotle had been so absorbed into the official teaching of the Church that it was defended as if it was part of the faith itself. This was exactly the point made by Galileo's contemporary Descartes, who commented that "theology has been so subjected to Aristotle that it is almost impossible to explain another philosophy without it seeming at first contrary to the Faith." Aristotle's universe portrayed a stationary earth at the center of the universe surrounded by a series of concentric spheres round which the moon, sun, planets and stars moved majestically. Of course, as we have already noted, such a cosmology is not found in the Bible, but the Roman Catholic Church at the time of Galileo defended the philosophy vigorously in the face of Galileo's espousal of Copernicus.

Some of Galileo's critics tried to use scriptural verses to attack the Copernican position. For example, the philosophers from Pisa drew attention to passages such as Psalm 93:3, which states that "The world is firmly established; it cannot be moved," claiming that this teaches that the earth must be physically immobile! Of course we would now see this verse in its context as what it is: a hymn of praise to the majesty and faithfulness of God in creation. And indeed that is how Galileo himself, who remained a faithful Catholic believer to the end of his days, tackled the question. Galileo even wrote a lengthy letter, later published as the *Letter to the Duchess Christina* (1615), in which he pointed out the dangers of mishandling scriptural passages in a way that took them out of context. Galileo's point is still as valid today as when he first wrote these words in his typically robust style:

> If I may speak my opinion freely, I should say further that it would perhaps fit in better with the decorum and majesty of the sacred writings to take measures for preventing every shallow and vulgar writer from giving to his compositions (often grounded upon foolish fancies) an air of authority by inserting in them passages from the Bible, interpreted (or rather distorted) into senses as far from the right meaning of scripture as those authors are near to absurdity who thus ostentatiously adorn their writings.

Galileo was much influenced by the stance of Augustine toward scripture who, back in the fourth century C.E., had warned Christians against the danger of being too literalistic in their biblical interpretations, thereby risking unnecessary conflict with contemporary "science" in a way that might make them look stupid.

It was to Galileo's credit that he refused to be bowed by the Inquisition and to the end of his days continued to insist that the evidence was overwhelming that the earth was in motion round the sun. Even though the Holy Office of the Inquisition pressured the aged Galileo "entirely to abandon the false opinion that the sun is the centre of the world and immovable, and that the earth is not the centre of the same and it moves," ever after Galileo was to maintain "*Eppur si muove*" (but still it moves): He had seen the evidence with his own eyes. It was this insistence of Galileo, on taking seriously the way the real world actually is, that led Einstein to comment that "because Galileo saw this, and particularly because he drummed it into the scientific world, he is the father of modern physics—indeed of modern science altogether."[8]

In retrospect we may see this unfortunate episode for what it was: a powerful institution inappropriately defending a secular philosophy in the name of faith, critiqued by one of the founders of the modern scientific movement whose grasp of scriptural interpretation was much sounder than that of his critics. For Galileo himself never considered that his scientific work stood in contradiction to his Christian faith, a point well illustrated by a comment he wrote to a French colleague after he had been found guilty of heresy:

> I have two sources of perpetual comfort, first, that in my writings there cannot be found the faintest shadow of irreverence towards the Holy Church; and second, the testimony of my own conscience, which only I and God in Heaven thoroughly know. And He knows that in this cause for which I suffer, though many might have spoken with more learning, none, not even the ancient Fathers, have spoken with more piety or with greater zeal for the Church than I.

There is much that we can learn from the Galileo episode about how to relate science and faith. One important lesson is that we should not press biblical passages out of their context to make them acquire meanings that the author never intended. Such reflections are relevant to the contemporary claims of the so-called "Young Earth Creationists" who claim biblical support for an age of the earth of 10,000 years in contrast to scientific evidence for an age of more than 4,500 million years. If there were only one or two scientific observations that suggested an age of thousands of millions of years, we could justifiably hold loose to the presumption of an ancient earth. But in fact, there are dozens of independent ways of measuring the age of the earth which give consistent results; furthermore, the same physical constants that are used in geological dating of rocks are lynchpins in disciplines as diverse as biology, biochemistry, astronomy, particle physics and chemistry. It is the same physics that is used to build the machine that screens for breast cancer at a hospital as is used to date a piece of ancient rock from Greenland. We cannot in this case ignore one piece of evidence, such as the age of the rock, without bringing a huge interlocking area of quite diverse science crashing down.

How do the "Young Earth Creationists" interpret scripture? Young Earth ideas come from the book of Genesis—by adding up the years for the genealogies and then assuming that the "days" mentioned in Genesis chapter 1 refer to literal days of 24 hours. But the Genesis accounts are perfectly compatible with an ancient universe. The thrust of the creation account in the Bible is that God created the universe purposefully, in an orderly fashion, and with one of God's major objectives to make it a place in which humans could live and have loving relationships with God. Even within the first few chapters of Genesis there are several different literary styles, a fact that should make us cautious in our interpretations. For example, Genesis 1:1–2:3 is clearly written in a different style from Genesis 2:3–4:26. Genesis 1:1–2:3 reads very like a theological essay or manifesto that stands as a grand introduction to the biblical story of salvation, laying down the "ground rules" for God's relationship to creation in general and to humankind in particular. To interpret such a passage as if it were a scientific narrative is simply to miss the point of the inspired writer. In his great commentary on Genesis published in 391 C.E. Augustine wrote with regard to Genesis chapter 1: "No Christian would dare say that the narrative must not be taken in a figurative sense." And another early Christian scholar of the Greek Church, Origen, commented in 231 C.E. on certain expressions used in the early chapters of Genesis, saying that, "I do not think anyone will doubt that these are figurative expressions which indicate mysteries through a semblance of history." The interpretation of Genesis chapter 1 as a "theological essay" is no modern invention but has been an accepted way of understanding the passage down through the centuries of Christian commentary. Those who want to read more about this will find the subject covered in greater depth in *Rebuilding the Matrix* (Lion, 2001).

The best currently determined scientific dates for the age of the universe, the age of the earth, and some of the most significant milestones in the evolution of life on earth are shown in Table 1. As with most scientific results, these dates are not likely to be the absolute final word—as scientific dating methods are refined, the ages will probably be tweaked. And finding the oldest fossil specimen of some particular species is a bit like trying to find the smallest giant in the world. However, the main features are unlikely to change much. One of the most striking points shown by Table 1 is that life existed on earth almost as soon as the environmental conditions made it possible to do so: almost the oldest rocks that have been discovered show evidence of carbon-based life. And ever since that time, through thousands of millions of years, the conditions on earth have remained favorable for such life to continue. This is quite remarkable, because life as we know it requires a relatively narrow band of environmental conditions to survive. For example, if the temperature of the earth's surface were to increase to above 100°C, as has indeed happened on other planets, all the water would boil off and that

A brief history of the universe

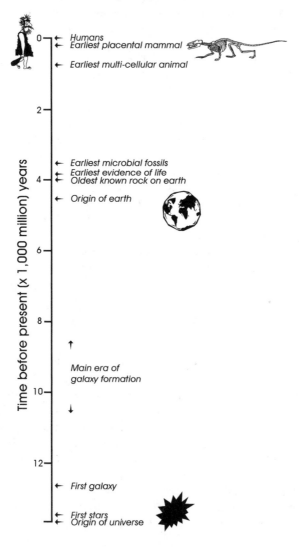

would be the end of life as we know it. We can take this either as an amazing coincidence, or from a Christian standpoint, as an example of God's providence in continually upholding and sustaining the world as a place fit for life. We will look in Chapter 6 in more detail at the inter-relatedness between all living organisms, and at ideas of creation and evolution from a biological perspective.

Table 1: Significant dates in the history of the universe

	Years before present
Origin of the universe (from microwave background radiation)[9]	13,700 ± 200 million
Origin of the solar system (= origin of earth)[10]	4,566 ± 2 million
Completion of earth's accretion[11]	4,510–4,450 million
Oldest known minerals on earth (zircon grains from Yilgarn craton, western Australia)[12]	4,404 ± 8 million
Oldest known rock on earth (Acasta gneiss, northwest Canada)[13]	4,000 million
Earliest evidence of life on earth (carbon isotope fractionation, from Akilia, southwest Greenland)[14]	3,850 million
Earliest microbial fossils on earth (microbial biofilms, stromatolites)[15]	3,500 million
Earliest known multicellular animal (Ediacaran faunas)[16]	575 million
Earliest known eutherian (placental) mammal (Eomaia)[17]	125 million
Earliest hominid (*Australopithecus*)[18]	c. 5 million
Early modern *Homo sapiens* (from Herto, Middle Awash, Ethiopia)[19]	160,000–154,000
Birth of Christ (comet, historical records, Bethlehem)[20]	9 March–4 May, 5 B.C.E.
Crucifixion of Christ (lunar eclipse, historical records, Jerusalem)[21]	Friday, 3 April, 33 C.E.

If the earth were one year old

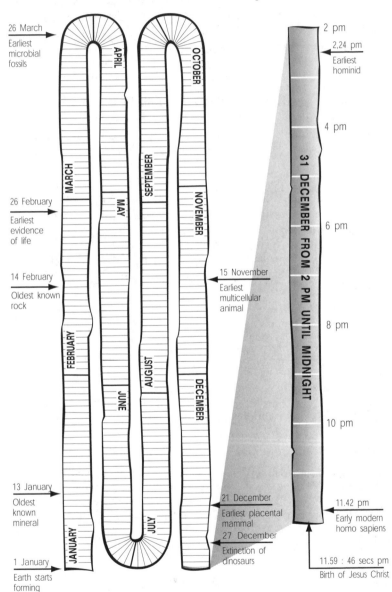

26 March
Earliest
microbial
fossils

26 February
Earliest
evidence
of life

14 February
Oldest known
rock

13 January
Oldest
known
mineral

1 January
Earth starts
forming

APRIL

MARCH

MAY

FEBRUARY

JUNE

JANUARY

JULY

OCTOBER

SEPTEMBER

NOVEMBER

AUGUST

DECEMBER

15 November
Earliest
multicellular
animal

21 December
Earliest placental
mammal

27 December
Extinction of
dinosaurs

31 DECEMBER FROM 2 PM UNTIL MIDNIGHT

2 pm

2,24 pm
Earliest
hominid

4 pm

6 pm

8 pm

10 pm

11.42 pm
Early modern
homo sapiens

11.59 : 46 secs pm
Birth of Jesus Christ

So can scientists believe the Bible? Certainly, providing they don't try the anachronistic approach of trying to read it as if it contains scientific literature, and providing they remember that the narratives are addressing very different kinds of question from those posed by science.

Are some research areas off-limits?

Media debates on both TV and radio that cover the topic of science and faith, or the ethical implications of new scientific findings, typically and quite correctly try to represent the various viewpoints. After involvement in many such programs, we can certainly discern a general trend. In most cases the producer brings the Christian in to the debate expecting that they will be the ones who want to slow down the pace of research, or to argue against the application of new technology, or to attack science in order to defend faith. When the program is actually recorded (or aired live—even better because then the "unexpected material" cannot be edited out), the producer is surprised to find that the Christian is often the most positive about science and its applications, whereas it is not uncommon to find that the atheist in the debate is less enthusiastic about the rapid progress of science. The New Age philosopher or Green activist in the debate is likely to be even more negative about science.

Those who have studied the history of the relationship between science and faith will not be surprised by such observations. Whereas, as we have already noted, the public perception of science-faith interactions is still strongly influenced by the so-called "conflict thesis," in reality the resonances between science and Christian faith are remarkably strong. So it is not surprising to see these attitudes displayed as Christians talk about their science. But of course this does raise a question, one which is as important for the public in general as it is for the scientific community—a question that faces everyone irrespective of their personal beliefs—and that is: How far should science go in understanding and manipulating the world around us?

From the perspective of Christian theology, it is clear that every aspect of God's universe is open to investigation. There are no signs up saying "Complex Brain: Do Not Investigate" or "Big Bang Theory: Danger" or "Origin of Species: Keep Out." If this is really God's universe, as Christians believe, then it is our duty to investigate how it works and to use our knowledge for the good of humankind.

Ethically, however, other factors certainly come into play. For example, some research may simply carry too high a risk of being used for evil ends, or too dangerous to make it appropriate for Christians to pursue. The eminent scientist and Astronomer Royal Sir Martin Rees believes that there is only a 50:50 chance of humankind surviving the twenty-first century. As the subtitle of his book *Our Final Century* indicates, he suggests that either "terror, error or environmental disaster" could spell the end for the human race.[22] Whether or not we accept this particular survival statistic, it is clear that the development of some scientific techniques is not morally neutral, and some may carry high risks. Playing with fire is often not a good idea.

Or another reason why some particular research may be off-limits is because the research itself may run counter to God's commands for the way that we should treat our fellow humans, or other living creatures. No one could argue that Mengele's infamous experiments forced on prisoners in Nazi concentration camps were justifiable, even though it is possible that some good may have come from them, such as understanding how to deal with some diseases that afflict humans. The God of the Bible makes it quite clear that the ends can never justify the means, if the things you have to do to achieve those ends are contrary to God's commandments.

The issues are much less clear-cut when there are obvious potential benefits of the research to humankind, but the experiments cause effects that we would otherwise prefer to avoid. An example might be whether we should purposefully modify animals in some way in an attempt to understand better how we may deal with analogous problems (such as mental incapacity or cancer) found in humans. In these difficult cases, biblical perspectives can be extremely helpful in finding an ethically acceptable way forward, not in the sense that the Bible gives a blueprint for what to do or not do in specific cases, but rather sets of guidelines that can impinge on particular ethical dilemmas. In the biblical worldview, God has placed us as stewards of creation, in some sense acting on God's behalf in our nurture and care for the created world. God has also made it clear that, although God values highly the life of even such a seemingly insignificant thing as a single sparrow, and not one dies without God's knowledge,[23] still God cares for humans even more. So on this basis we may perhaps be justified in using animals for medical research, but not for testing whether yet another cosmetic causes skin irritation. But we have to ensure throughout such research that the animals suffer as little as possible, that they are cared for humanely, and that the experiments are designed and constructed to the best of our ability so as to minimize the numbers of animals that are used and the extent of their suffering. Indeed, it is precisely such factors that are used as criteria by the Home Office in the United Kingdom when deciding whether a scientist should be issued with a license in order to carry out experiments using animals. Similar ethical factors to these come into play in many other contexts, such as the testing of new drugs in "double-blind" experiments on humans.

It is often difficult for non-scientific members of the general public to understand the technical issues involved in making decisions about whether or not to pursue particular areas of research. This has sometimes led to a degree of arrogance by scientists in assuming that they know best, and essentially in writing off the concerns of non-scientists as based on ignorance or lack of understanding. However, there is a strong case to be made that if the science is something that has the potential to benefit other people, then society at large ought to be supportive of the application of that science. The teaching of Jesus is that we should love our neighbour as we love ourselves, which means that we are at fault if we deliberately withhold benefits from our neighbour.

At the end of the day, scientific knowledge, like any other kind of knowledge, can be used for good or for evil. So, yes, Christians think that we should investigate every nook and cranny of God's good creation, but we had better make sure that the new knowledge is used wisely and not arrogantly.

Use of the world's resources

An attitude of arrogant domination toward the world around us is subverted by the biblical idea of "stewardship." The concept of stewardship is ingrained in the creation order from the earliest times: in Genesis chapter 2 we are told that it was the task of humankind to care for the rest of creation and that they were placed in a garden, the Garden of Eden, "to work it and to take care of it."[24] Sustainable consumption, the idea that we are accountable to future generations to leave the world in more than just a barely habitable state, is a popular viewpoint at the beginning of the twenty-first century. For the first time in the history of the world, the earth's population may be approaching a sustainable limit, so such a perspective is an important, perhaps even an essential one, for pragmatic as well as ethical reasons. It is also clear that science is a crucial ally in developing strategies and technologies for sustainable development. We shall return in Chapter 8 to a fuller discussion of sustainability from a Christian perspective.

But the Christian view encompasses more than just the desirability of sustainable consumption. God specifically gave humankind responsibility for his creation, with the command to use it for the good of others. This is not the woolly, feel-good attitude that says it would be wonderful if we could all return to a rural agrarian economy and get rid of our TVs and computer games. The Christian perspective is that we should harness science and the innate fruitfulness of the created order to improve the lot of humankind. It is certainly desirable that medical care should be improved worldwide; that people should not only have enough to eat, but should be bountifully supplied with food, as are we in the high income countries; that people should not freeze at night or roast by day, but should have sufficient energy to heat or cool their homes; and so on through a myriad of other things that collectively we class as quality of life. If provision of sufficient energy to provide a good quality of life for everyone means that we should develop nuclear energy, then that is, in principle, a good goal for Christian endeavor.

This robustly positive view toward the utilization of the created order for the common good is balanced within Christian theology by an element of realism that arises out of the doctrine of the Fall. This refers to the fact that humankind is not living in the state that God first intended. Far from living lives in which God's priorities are central, humankind has decided to become autonomous and to set up its own moral standards and ways of doing things. So the first fatal consequence of the Fall is that relationships both between people, and between humans and God, have been tainted and damaged by the prevalent tendency to sinfulness, to self-interest. The practical outworking of this is that working together for the common good of others is made more difficult. Yet of course most stewardship issues involve corporate responsibilities, and the realization that what I do affects other people.

One of the clearest contemporary examples of this is the issue of the emission of greenhouse gases: at an individual level, the car I drive to the shops, the carnations I buy as a present, which have been flown in from Africa to Atlanta the previous day, or the computer screen I carelessly leave switched on overnight, all use energy which in some measure causes degradation of the environment for people living elsewhere; at a national level, the energy policies that our government implements, the way it taxes our gasoline and our industry, and our holiday travel all affect the pollution that we allow to circulate through the atmosphere and hydrosphere to other nations around the world. The difficulty of getting even a small measure of international agreement on the global climate change protocols points up the magnitude of the task of overcoming self-interest for the long-term common good. Added to the innate tendency of humans to put self-interest first is the difficulty of communicating across cultural and language barriers,[25] which easily translates into suspicion of other's motives.

Fortunately, central to the Christian worldview is also the fact of redemption. Christ's sacrificial death on the cross was a pivotal point in history at which human sinfulness was decisively dealt with by God's love for us, thereby reversing the catastrophic effects of the Fall. The cross on which Jesus died therefore acts like a bridge to enable people to come back once more into a personal relationship with God. Personal redemption leads, or should lead, to a positive impact on the environment. As humans are restored to being the kinds of "stewards" of God's resources that God originally intended, so the earth is also redeemed as the effects of the Fall are reversed. The Christian worldview therefore provides a powerful motivation to care for the world and its resources, although it has to be admitted that Christians have often failed to take this teaching sufficiently seriously to affect their lifestyles and their over-consumption.

Science encounters faith

The public perception of "science encountering faith" is sometimes one of hostility and conflict. Yet in this chapter we have been mapping out a very different kind of territory. It is one in which the creation of God's good material world is foundational to the scientific endeavor. The theistic universe is congenial to the scientific enterprise. It is marked by coherence and reproducibility, essential properties for the practice of science. Exploring God's created order is part of a Christian's worship. The beauty displayed all around us in the properties of matter is given an extra dimension by the knowledge that it points to the wisdom of the all-powerful creator. The responsible stewardship of this remarkable planet is intimately bound up with the idea that we are made in God's image.

Part II

Hot Issues for the Twenty-First Century

CHAPTER 6

Created or Evolved?

If the twentieth century was the century of physics then it seems likely that the twenty-first century will be the century of biology. One of the main reasons for thinking this is the increasing power of molecular genetics to analyze living organisms at the molecular level. The Human Genome Project has obtained a complete sequence of human DNA and the genome sequences of other organisms are now becoming available at an increasing pace. It is already possible to compare the DNA sequence of every human gene with the equivalent gene found in many other species.

Whereas physics has been going through a rather non-mechanistic phase, particularly following the advent of quantum theory, biology is in the midst of the reverse process, in which the focus is on the interactions between molecules, and the way in which these define the properties of the whole organism ("how genotype determines phenotype in a given environment"). Through the insights of biochemistry and molecular biology, living matter is now amenable to investigation and manipulation in ways that would have been unthinkable even a few decades ago. Advances in biology are certainly likely to raise some hot issues for the twenty-first century.

Creation and evolution

One topic that has more of a nineteenth than a twenty-first century ring to it is that of creation and evolution.[1] Given that nineteenth-century Christian thinkers felt that they had given this topic a good airing, and that they had reached some quite satisfactory conclusions that did justice to both science and the Bible, it is rather surprising to note how the debate was revived during the course of the twentieth century and still remains active today. There are some particular historical reasons for this that are of interest.

One reason appears to be Christian reaction, particularly in the US, to the horrors of the First World War. The Kaiser's philosophy of "might is right" in Germany drew heavily on the idea of the "survival of the fittest," a concept that had been introduced into Darwinian theory by Herbert Spencer. Much to Darwin's disgust, Spencer had popularized evolution during the late nineteenth century as if it represented a grand philosophy for the whole of life, history and human progress, rather than in its straightforward Darwinian form of a biological theory to explain the origins of biological diversity. The fact that Darwinian theory had been utilized to support Germany's military ambitions was publicized in the US by several books that had a great influence on William Jennings Bryan, a three-time defeated Democratic candidate for the presidency of the United States, a Presbyterian layman and one of the greatest populist reformers of that era.[2] Bryan tapped into a public concern that militaristic ideas would spread from Western Europe to America, and that evolution would "sap the morality of the nation's youth." Armed with such an understanding of the scope of evolution, Bryan proceeded to campaign vigorously against evolution in the name of creationism.

The creationist movement that Bryan supported during the 1920s eventually fizzled out, but was revived again in the US with great vigor during the 1960s, and once again was linked to a concern that evolution was in some sense immoral. Numerous court cases were fought in an attempt to prevent the teaching of evolution in American schools. Henry Morris, president of the Institute for Creation Research, suggested that the acceptance of the theory of evolution was responsible, among other things, for promiscuity, pornography and perversion.[3] In this brand of creationism it was maintained that the earth was made some 10,000 years ago over a period of six days of 24 hours each, and that each species was created by God separately, so denying the claim fundamental to evolutionary theory that there is a unity between all living organisms.

In contrast to the creationists, other Christians such as Teilhard de Chardin and Frank Tipler tried to use evolution to support grand religious schemes pointing to the evolution of life toward an eventual perfected "omega point" (we have already discussed the shortcomings of such schemes in Chapter 2). On the other side of the religious fence, atheists such as Richard Dawkins have tried to use the theory of evolution to prop up their view that our existence on planet earth has no ultimate meaning. Because atheistic writers such as Dawkins try to use evolution to support a materialistic philosophy, in response Christian apologists such as Phillip E. Johnson[4] have proposed that Christians should attack evolution because they believe it is intrinsically atheistic.

Besides being used in both religious and anti-religious arguments, at various times evolution has also been used to support capitalism, communism and racism, not to speak of numerous other "isms"!

From such observations it will immediately be apparent that a key confusion that frequently occurs when "creation" and "evolution" are being discussed is that the people in conversation often have quite different definitions in mind as to what these words actually mean. The participants can then spend a lot of time talking at cross-purposes and generating heat rather than light. There is an important difference between the biological theory of evolution and the various philosophies that people have tried to derive from it ever since the time of Darwin. The fact that many of these philosophies are mutually exclusive should alert us to the possibility that none of them is logically based on the biological theory of evolution, but rather are parasitic upon it. Study of the history of science illustrates many examples of the ways in which scientific theories, particularly the "grand theories" of science, have been used for ideological purposes. The common strategy is to insinuate, using dubious arguments, or repeated statements, that a particular ideology is closely associated with a particular scientific theory. All kinds of ideas can then hitch a ride along with the grand theories of science, until they become weighed down by the accretion of associated ideologies. The theory of evolution has often suffered such a fate. To have a sensible discussion about creation and evolution, we must therefore first spend some time unwrapping the meanings of these terms.

Biological evolution

The purpose of this section is not to consider the evidence for and against evolution per se—this discussion can be surveyed in any good university textbook of biology. The aim rather is to understand what biologists mean when they talk about evolution. By the contemporary use of the term "evolution," biologists are referring to a process that results in heritable changes in a population spread over many generations. Heritable changes occur by means of genes. A gene is a hereditary unit that can be passed on unaltered for many generations. The gene pool is the set of all genes in a species or population. So when biologists say that they have observed evolution, they mean that they have detected a change in the frequency of genes in a population. The process of evolution can be succinctly summarized in three short phrases: genes mutate; individuals are selected; populations evolve.

Evolution can therefore occur without morphological change, that is without any visible changes in the overall structure or appearance of an organism. Equally, morphological change can occur without evolution. For example, humans are larger now than in the recent past, a result of better diet, not a result of genetic changes. Evolution only refers to those changes that are inherited.

In order for evolution to occur, that is, for heritable changes in a population spread over many generations, there must be mechanisms to increase or create genetic variation and mechanisms to decrease it. When people talk about evolution they often confuse the phenomenon itself with the mechanisms invoked to explain it.

One important mechanism that decreases genetic variation is natural selection. Some individuals within a population leave more offspring than others. Over time, the genes from these reproductively more prolific or successful individuals will become over-represented in the population compared with earlier generations. This difference in reproductive capability is called natural selection. The most common action of natural selection is to remove unfit genetic variants as they arise via mutation. Natural selection acts as a stringent sieve to prevent the passing on of genes that are deleterious to the reproductive success of an organism. However, occasionally mutant genes will bestow a reproductive advantage, in which case genetic variation will be maintained. Overall, therefore, natural selection acts to reduce genetic variation, or in some cases to maintain genetic variation in a population, but as a mechanism it is never the origin of variation. It is largely a conservative force.

There are plenty of examples of how natural selection operates in contemporary human populations. One example is the maintenance of mutant genes in the human gene pool in parts of the world where malaria is endemic. If one form of the gene is mutated, whereas the second copy is normal, then such individuals are more resistant to malaria. A double-dose of the mutant gene, such as that for sickle-cell anemia, is definitely bad for you, but if you have a single copy of the mutant gene then your reproductive fitness is increased relative to people who have no mutant genes at all.

Three different mechanisms can increase genetic variation within a lineage. Every cell division involves the duplication of its DNA. As millions of our cells divide every second, each individual produces thousands of miles every minute of newly copied DNA. The cellular machinery that copies DNA sometimes (though extremely rarely) makes mistakes, which alters the sequence of a gene. This is called a mutation. Mutations can also increase as a result of chemical contamination or ra-

How evolution works

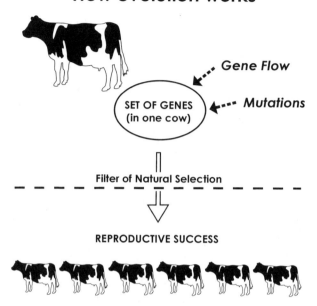

diation. There are many kinds of mutation. For example a point mutation involves the substitution of one nucleotide base in the DNA
sequence by a different nucleotide, and in some cases this leads to a
change in a single amino acid in the encoded protein. In other cases a
stop signal can be introduced by the mutation so that only part of the
gene is read into a protein sequence, and the protein that results is
truncated, rather like a sentence which is chopped in half.

Most mutations are neutral with regard to reproductive fitness.
Only a small proportion of the DNA of multicellular organisms actually
encodes for genes—in humans it is about 2 percent. Other sections of
our DNA are involved in the regulation of gene expression (the actual
making of the protein that the gene encodes), while the function of the
rest of our DNA is not yet well understood. So most mutations occur in
the 98 percent of our DNA that doesn't encode genes. Even when mutations appear in the DNA that encodes genes, most are lost from the gene
pool since they make no difference to reproductive success. Most mutations that have any "phenotypic" effect—that is, that make any difference to the organism—are deleterious. Only a very small percentage of
mutations is beneficial, that is, increase the reproductive fitness of the
organism: but of course it is precisely these mutations that are statisti-
cally more likely to be passed on. A mutant allele (a variant form of the

same gene) that confers a 1 percent increase in fitness has only a 2 percent chance of becoming fixed in the population. Yet it is this tiny proportion of beneficial alleles that provides novelty and scope for change as part of the process of generating biological diversity.

One example of a beneficial mutant allele comes from the mosquito. In this organism a mutant gene arose by chance which conferred the ability to break down the type of organophosphates commonly used in insecticides. Not surprisingly this mutant gene rapidly swept through the worldwide mosquito population, thereby providing resistance to such insecticides, a good example of evolution in progress. Clearly this particular mutation has been of greater benefit to mosquitoes than it has to humans.

The other two mechanisms, besides mutation, that increase genetic variation are *recombination*—the exchange of genes between the mother's and father's chromosomes that occurs during the formation of gametes (sperm and eggs), and *gene flow*—the introduction of new genes into a population by migration of another population.

So far we have considered only evolution within a biological lineage, that is, within a single species. What about speciation? A species refers to a population of organisms which interbreed with each other but not with other organisms. Speciation is thought to occur either by *allopatric mechanisms,* which happen when a population is split into two (or more) geographically divided subdivisions that organisms cannot bridge (such as the formation of a new ocean separating two landmasses as a result of continental drift), or by *sympatric mechanisms,* which occur when two subpopulations become reproductively isolated without first becoming geographically isolated.

Some biologists think that special mechanisms, different from those that we have considered so far, may be involved in speciation, whereas others believe that in many cases the molecular mechanisms that have been described so far are adequate to account for reproductive isolation. The issue awaits a clear resolution. Genetically, the reasons for reproductive isolation may in some cases be quite trivial in comparison with the much greater degree of genetic diversity that exists within a species. For example, in a sympatric form of speciation a mutation might occur in a key developmental gene that regulates some aspect of reproduction so that successful mating can only occur within the population that shares the mutant allele. Speciation may result from something as trivial as a change in plumage color, or the inability of a bird to learn the correct mating song from its parents—no song, no sex—or the formation of a new mountain range between a population of snails that used to interbreed. When the two populations finally get back together again after a few millions of years in isolation, it may often happen that their accumulation of mutant alleles now means that they can no longer interbreed.

Until recently it was difficult to identify genes that might be specifically involved in speciation. However, the use of organisms that multiply quickly, like fruit flies, coupled with rapid sequencing techniques and the power of computer programs to compare gene sequences, is changing the situation. For example if attempts are made to breed the fruit fly *Drosophila simulans* with another species of fruit fly called *Drosophila melanogaster,* then the male hybrid offspring die. Recently this has been shown to be due to a gene (called *Nup96*) on chromosome 3 of *D. simulans* that interacts with one or more unknown genes on the *D. melanogaster* male X chromosome to cause the death of the offspring.[5] So it is likely to be this particular gene that contributes to the reproductive barrier between these two species. In fact sequencing of the *Nup96* gene from many individuals from both species has revealed important interspecies differences in the sequence between the two species. Since differences in gene sequence translate into differences in protein structure and properties, this probably explains the incompatibility of the *D. simulans* version of the gene when in the presence of the *D. melanogaster* X chromosome. So in this case it is quite likely that accumulating mutations in a single gene were sufficient to precipitate the branching of two separate lineages.

Many other factors, also, may be involved in speciation events, not least the succession of catastrophes that are thought to have wiped out large proportions of species at various times during the earth's history. The largest mass extinction came at the end of the Permian period about 250 million years ago when as many as 96 percent of all species are thought to have become extinct, and the most famous one occurred at the end of the Cretaceous period, about 60 million years ago, when the dinosaurs were wiped out. Mass extinctions like these were followed by periods of radiation when new species evolve to fill the empty ecological niches left behind. It has been estimated that there are about 20 million species alive today, but in contrast about 2 billion species have come into being and then gone extinct during the history of our planet.

Speciation is easiest to study in lakes and on islands where the environment is highly restricted.[6] For example, until very recently there were more than 170 species of cichlid fish in Lake Victoria in Africa and initially it was thought that these all evolved from a single species of fish since the lake's origin about 750,000 years ago in the mid-Pleistocene era. However, more recently genetic and geological studies have revealed

Speciation by isolation

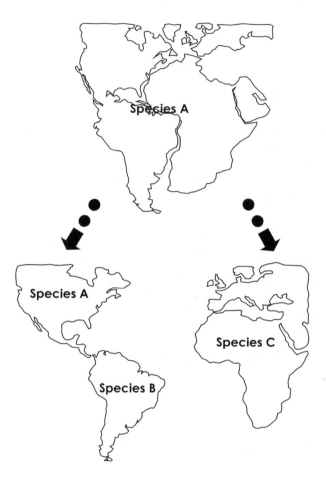

a more complex picture.[7] Geological evidence suggests that the lake dried out completely about 14,700 years ago and that it was then "seeded" by two distinct lineages of cichlid fish from the more ancient Lake Kivu. Irrespective of the precise sequence of events, the large number of cichlid species found until recently in Lake Victoria provides a striking example of rapid speciation in action. The different species show differences in morphology (body structure and appearance) which are linked to their feeding habits. For example, virtually every major food source in the lake is exploited by one species or another. Some cichlids eat insects, others crustaceans, others eat plants, and yet others molluscs. Each new species has found their particular ecological niche. In fact one species, H. welcommei, has the odd habit of feeding on fish scales that it scrapes off the tails of other fish! Just 4,000 years ago a small new lake called Lake Nabugabo became isolated from Lake Victoria by a narrow sandbar and this lake already has seven different cichlid species, five of which are not found in Lake Victoria and which therefore probably evolved during these past 4,000 years. The Lake Nabugabo species vary most from the Lake Victoria species in male color. So the cichlid species of these two lakes provides a vivid example of the way in which speciation can be rapid (in terms of geological time) and abundant, given the right environment.

It is sometimes thought that speciation events must involve the evolution of completely new genes. This is also a mistaken idea. We are all living fossils in the sense that our genes have extremely ancient roots. When we compare ourselves with mice, a species from which we split genetically less than 75 million years ago, then we find that 99 percent of our genes are shared with mice, not in the sense that they are identical, but in the sense that they are so similar that they must encode similar or identical proteins. In most cases those proteins carry out in the mouse the same set of tasks as they perform in humans. In recent evolution, that is, evolution that has occurred during the past 600 million years, it is not the generation of completely new genes that has been the key mechanism driving evolutionary change, but the reorganization and refining of genes already in existence. To use an analogy from architecture, the myriad forms of building that characterize the city of Cambridge come mainly not from the use of different types of stone and brick, but from different configurations of similar bricks and stones.

A lot of the novelty generated during evolution appears to come from gene duplication. Occasionally a gene is duplicated as a cell divides so that two copies of that gene are integrated into the genome of the daughter cells instead of the original one. If this occurs in the germ-line cells (sperm or eggs) then the gene-duplication event will be passed on to the progeny. Sometimes the new gene ends up in a different part of the genome so that its regulation is different, or it may not even be expressed as a protein at all.[8] Recent studies have shown that as many as 50 percent of our own genes have arisen in evolution as a result of gene duplication.[9] This is almost certainly an underestimate, because many of the duplicated genes are eventually lost from the genome (because they are not really needed), or else end up becoming pseudo-genes (genes that are no longer functional). For example, our own chromosome 7 encodes 1,150 genes, but also 941 pseudo-genes, which lie there like molecular fossils of our evolutionary past.[10]

So gene duplication represents a "quick-and-easy" mechanism to drive evolution. The second copy of the gene may be under different selection constraints from the original copy. This means that its gene sequence can start drifting faster due to accumulating mutations, endowing the protein with similar but not identical properties to those it had before.

But increases in gene number alone do not account for increases in morphological complexity.[11] The simple nematode worm possesses nearly 20,000 genes but lacks the full range of cell types seen in the fruit fly which contains fewer than 14,000 genes. Vertebrates have only about twice as many genes as invertebrates, despite their greater range of tissue types and increased complexity of structure. The key factor in evolution seems to be the changes that occur in the DNA regulatory sequences that control the panoply of genes that are switched on or off during development.[12] As many as 10 percent of our own 30,000 genes are transcription factors—proteins that regulate gene expression. It has also been calculated that perhaps twice as much human non-coding DNA is facing selection pressure during genetic change as compared with the coding regions (those DNA sequences that actually encode proteins). So it seems likely that in many cases speciation will be found to involve changes in a whole panoply of regulatory DNA sequences in addition to genes that encode proteins.

In science, theories tend to get discarded unless they continue to fit the data. Most biologists do not work on evolutionary theory per se but rather carry out their research within the evolutionary paradigm. And what they find in practice is that the theory is like a work-horse that continues to make sense of the data and so they go on believing in it. For example, the sequencing of human DNA, a consequence of the Human Genome Project, has provided data that makes perfect sense within evolutionary theory.

Now what you expect if all living organisms have a shared evolutionary history is that many genes will be found in common between organisms, but that the differences in the sequences of genes, and indeed in the actual genes utilized, will increase in proportion to evolutionary time. In other words, the longer it was since one organism shared a common ancestor with another, the more time there will be for genes to change or to be used in novel ways. But if the genes are really essential to life as they are, then there'll be a strong selection pressure to keep them the same way. Remember that natural selection is a very conservative force, preventing change.

One of the remarkable findings from a comparison between the genomes of humans, worms, flies and yeast is just how similar we all are, and yet there are some significant differences as well. In our bodies we have about 500 genes for kinases—enzyme proteins that regulate almost every aspect of our body's functions—which means that nearly 2 percent of all our genes belongs to just this one class of enzyme. Now you can divide all of the family of kinases up into 209 subfamilies, based on similarities between the gene sequences. There are 93 families that are shared between humans, flies and worms and a further 51 families that are shared between humans, flies, worms and yeast. So we actually contain thousands of genes that are present also in yeast and that have not changed that much since our evolutionary path split off from yeast about 1 billion years ago. And we share even more genes with the lowly worm and the fly, from which we split off in the so-called Cambrian explosion about 600 million years ago. So genes are like molecular fossils, telling us much about our evolutionary histories.[13]

The biblical doctrine of creation

Having spent some time outlining the key elements in biological evolution, we can now consider how it relates to the biblical doctrine of

Sharing a common genetic history – the example of kinases

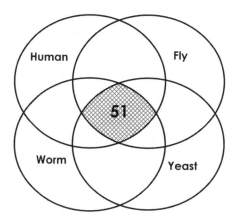

Figure 11: This represents the 51 shared sub-families of the enzymes known as kinases that are shared in common between humans, flies, worms and yeast.

creation. We have already noted in Chapter 5 that Christians are robust theists: they believe that God is intimately involved in creating and sustaining every aspect of the universe in all its details. Creation is a seamless cloth of God's activity. Just as the existence of the TV drama depends upon the continual targeting of electrons on to the TV screen to generate the necessary images—and there would be no drama if the flow of electrons ceased—so there would be no scientists and nothing for scientists to describe were God to cease his ongoing creative and sustaining activity.

Within this biblical framework the term "creation" refers not to a particular mechanism for explaining the origins of biological diversity, but to the relationship between God and everything that exists. The Bible uses the Hebrew or Greek words translated "create" or "form" or "made" with a wide range of nuances, just as those words carry a similar range of meanings in the English language today. The word translated "create" in many biblical texts is clearly used to refer to processes such as: the creation of the people of Israel; or to the creation of the New Jerusalem; or to the creation of new animals that takes place during the normal process of animal birth;[14] or to the creation of light and darkness that God does every day in the normal passage from day to night.[15] The modern tendency to look for God at the boundaries of our present knowledge is quite alien to biblical thought. When God is pictured as answering Job out of the storm while Job was struggling with the problem of evil (Job 38), it is to the whole gamut of God's creative activity that he draws attention, not merely to big things like the "laying of earth's foundations" (verse 4) and organizing the stars (verses 31–33), but also to its more mundane aspects like watering deserts (verses 25–26), frost formation (verse 29) and providing food for lions (verse 39).

The concept of "creation" is not therefore in any sense a *rival* to the biological theory of evolution. Evolution can simply be viewed as the mechanism that God chooses to bring biological diversity into being. The word "creation" refers to the origin and ongoing nature of that process. So the biblical concept of creation refers not to a description of the particular *mechanisms* that God has chosen to bring biological diversity into being, because creation is not a concept that refers to mechanisms, but to God's immanent ongoing creative relationship with the whole universe, including its biological diversity. "Creation" is not therefore a scientific term at all and makes no pretense to be so—rather it is a theological term expressing a prior belief about God's actions, a framework within which all of our scientific observations and descriptions are then interpreted.

The atheist Richard Dawkins appears to be under the impression that when Christians talk about "creation" they are referring to some rival theory to evolution. It is unfortunate that the word "creationist" has become attached to a group of people who have a certain view as to how biological diversity was created by God, whereas it would be much more accurate to attach the word to anybody who believes in God as creator, irrespective of their beliefs about how God created. Unfortunately, however, words are defined by their usage, and the term "creationist" has indeed become attached to those who disbelieve evolution. Therefore insofar as Dawkins is contrasting evolutionary theory with creationist beliefs, he is correct to suggest that these are rival theories about the origins of biological diversity: in the evolutionary theory there is an unbroken lineage between all living organisms from their earliest beginnings to the present day; in the other theory, the creationist view, there are discontinuities in which God supposedly created each species separately. One could argue that as long as there are creationists around, so will there be clones of Richard Dawkins around, because as long as different groups of people invest scientific theories with rival ideologies, then so long will those disputes feed on each other and indeed benefit from each other in a synergistic way.

The adoption of a robust, biblically based theism, however, evacuates evolutionary theory of any kind of philosophical pretensions, least of all of any claim to be an argument for a materialistic philosophy. Science is about truth-telling and, if Darwinian evolution is currently the best explanation we have to explain how biological diversity came into being—and biologists certainly think it is—then we should be at the forefront in telling the truth about God's world. Occasionally popular writers, even Christian writers, suggest that evolutionary theory is under some kind of crisis within the scientific community. This is not true. In recent years the theory has been enormously strengthened by the advent of molecular genetics. The theory is so powerful because it links together disparate data from a wide range of scientific disciplines, including zoology, anatomy, biochemistry, molecular biology, geology, paleontology, anthropology and ecology. There is no alternative rival theory on offer at the present time. Christians should therefore be truth-tellers when it comes to accurately describing the convictions of the current generation of biological scientists.

Once it is understood that evolution is a description of God's creative activity, then any supposed conflict between creation and evolution simply dissolves. There is nothing "naturalistic" or "materialistic" about describing how God's material world operates. It should be noted that such a stance undermines the use of scientific theories as arenas for ideological conflict. Instead it places the emphasis of the conflict, such as that between atheists and Christians, on the competing metaphysical convictions adopted by these protagonists.

Many Christians from the time of Darwin until the present day have held the view that God has created all living organisms by a long process of evolution. In the light of those today who think that evolution has atheistic implications, it is interesting to note that back in the nineteenth century Darwinian evolution was accepted rather quickly by all the mainstream Christian denominations in the United States and Great Britain—within a few decades of the publication of *The Origin of Species* in 1859. The idea, so loved by the media, that Darwinism was locked in a bitter battle with the Church from its inception, has long ago been picked apart by revisionist historians, and the picture that has emerged is both more complex and more intriguing. The British historian James Moore writes that "with but few exceptions the leading Christian thinkers in Britain and America came to terms quite readily with Darwinism and evolution,"[16] and the American sociologist George Marsden reports that " . . . with the exception of Harvard's Louis Agassiz, virtually every American Protestant zoologist and botanist accepted some form of evolution by the early 1870s."[17]

Ironically, in light of the fact that today about half the population of the United States disbelieves the theory of evolution, in the nineteenth century it was Christian academics who did much to popularize the theory in the country. For example Asa Gray, Professor of Natural History at Harvard, an orthodox Presbyterian in belief, had long been Darwin's confidant, and was one of the privileged few to receive advance complimentary copies of *The Origin of Species*. Gray reviewed the book very favorably in the US and arranged for its publication there in 1860.[18]

To address all of the issues raised by the theory of evolution is beyond the scope of this book. However, we will briefly consider the question of how God's creative actions are compatible with the role of chance in evolution, since this well illustrates how robust theism can provide a framework in which particular objections to evolution lose their potency.

Chance, evolution and creation

It is often thought that evolution involves a chance process and therefore must be in some way incompatible with a God of order and design. But a moment's thought will show that such a view is simplistic.

Consider, for example, the course of your life until now. If you are a Christian, then you believe that God's providential care has been sovereign over all the details of your life, even from the time before you were born. This includes the fact that one particular sperm fertilized one particular egg at a particular moment in time to generate that genetically unique individual that you became. Millions of sperm were involved in that race to get to the egg first—you could so easily have been of the opposite sex to what you are now, and you could easily have looked physically quite different. Fertilization is truly a chance process. Yet you still believe that God was sovereign in all these contingent events that brought you into existence.

Why stop at biology? If you are a Christian, think about all the myriad events that have been woven together in an immensely complex tapestry to bring about God's will in your life. Some of those events may have been painful—perhaps things that happened quite out of your control. Other events were quite mundane, yet made a profound difference to the course of your life. The film *Sliding Doors* was right—seemingly trivial differences in life can have enormous effects. At one level they represent chance events—there is no way that we or anyone else can predict them—but Christians also believe that God is ultimately in control of everything that happens.

The Bible is consistent in its teaching that events that many people would ascribe to chance are within the boundaries of God's sovereignty and plan. When the prophet Micaiah predicted that King Ahab would be killed in battle at Ramoth Gilead,[19] this indeed came to pass, but it happened because someone "drew his bow at random and hit the king of Israel between the sections of his armour."[20] As Proverbs 16:33 so vividly puts the point: "The lot is cast into the lap, but its every decision is from the Lord." The Bible sees God's works occurring equally in all the various manifestations of his activity, whether in the more "law-like" workings of the natural world (Psalm 33:6–11), in chance events (Proverbs 16:33), or in his control of the weather (Psalm 148:8), which today we describe using chaos theory. There is never a hint in the Bible that certain types of event in the natural world are any more or any less the activity of God than other events.

But what do we mean by chance and how does that understanding relate to evolution? Unfortunately the word chance can be used with at least three quite distinct meanings and people are not always clear in discussion which meaning they have in mind. First, there is the kind of chance events that are predictable in principle but not in practice. For example, if we had enough information about each of the millions of sperm racing to fertilize an egg, then providing we had a complete description also of the environment, we could theoretically predict which one would win the race. But in the second kind of chance, that which typifies events at the quantum level, our ignorance about the future is complete. When a radioactive atom decays we have no way of knowing when the next high-energy particle will be emitted, and this reflects our inability to predict in principle and not just in practice. Some people call that kind of chance "pure chance." Then there is a third type of chance, which we can label "metaphysical chance." This is something very different from the other two types of chance and refers to the philosophy that in some ultimate sense the universe came into being "by chance" and has no real rhyme or reason.

Now as it happens it is only the first two types of chance that are relevant to evolution. The reason for this is that mutations can occur in DNA due to failures in the actions of DNA repair enzymes that occasionally miss errors during the "proofreading" process. This is an example of the first type of chance—it might be predictable in principle, but not in practice. But mutations in DNA can also happen by exposure to radiation—this is an example of the second type of chance, non-predictable in theory as well as in practice. But so far as evolutionary mechanisms are concerned, it really doesn't matter whether the mutation arose by the first or second kind of chance. Either way a change has come into being in the gene sequence, and if that change occurs in the germ-line cells so that it is passed on to the next generation, then the change will in any case be tested out by the "filter" of reproductive success.

So we can picture the evolutionary process taken as a whole as a two-stage process in which random mutations are generated in the genes in step one, but then in step two these changes are incredibly tightly controlled by the "filtering process" of reproductive success. Just how tight this filtering process is can readily be seen by comparing the 99 percent similarity in the genes between humans and mice, as outlined above. What this means is that even tiny changes in the gene sequence have been lethal, or at least markedly deleterious, not only to any mice that got them, but also to all the intervening mammals that characterize our evolutionary lineage ever since we branched off from mice. So scientists say that such genes are under a very strong "selection pressure" to stay the same. One little change and you are a dead mouse.

So if you look at the overall process of evolution, it is very far indeed from any notion of "metaphysical chance." It is a stringently regulated series of events in which food chains are built up in precisely defined ecological niches. The process has occurred in particular environments characterized by parameters such as cold and heat, light and darkness, wetness and dryness, with the constraints of gravity playing a key role in defining animal and plant sizes and shapes. There are good reasons why elephants don't fly. And there are good reasons why the eye has evolved not once but many times during the process of evolution.

Therefore evolutionary mechanisms are nothing like the processes that we normally think of as "random" in any ultimate sense. When your TV breaks down and you get a horrible, meaningless fuzz on your screen you might rightly think of that as "random noise" without ultimate meaning. But the biological diversity generated by the evolutionary process is as far from that type of random fuzz as you can imagine: it represents a highly organized collection of mechanisms that are only possible in a carbonaceous world with a particular set of elements and physical laws. The physical properties of the universe were defined in the very first few femto-seconds after the Big Bang, and the process of evolution depends utterly on that particular set of properties. Without them we would not be here.

So Christians see the evolutionary process simply as the way that God has chosen to bring biological diversity into being, including us. The process per se has no particular theological significance. That's the way things are and our task as scientists is to describe the way things are—what God has done in bringing this vast array of biological diversity into being. Of one thing we can be sure: the evolutionary process provides no grounds for thinking that the universe is a "chance" process in any ultimate metaphysical sense. In fact, quite the reverse. As biologists we marvel at the complexity and diversity of this planet's life forms, and at the fact that we as humans are indissolubly linked by our evolutionary history with every life form on earth.

It should also be obvious from these reflections that chance does nothing. Chance is simply a handy description that we humans use for our beliefs about the properties of matter. There is no such agent as "metaphysical chance," but there is the human belief held by some people that the universe has no ultimate meaning. However, those who try propping up that particular belief system using the prestige of scientific theories will find not a shred of comfort in evolutionary theory.

So there is really no need for evolution to be a hot issue for Christians, or for anyone else for that matter, in the twenty-first century. Darwin's Christian contemporaries in the nineteenth century had it just right when they decided to baptize Darwinian theory into the Christian doctrine of creation. There is no reason why we should not continue to do the same in the twenty-first century.

Darwin's Black Box?

A 1996 book by Michael Behe entitled *Darwin's Black Box*[21] illustrates rather well the way in which the attempt to revive a contemporary form of natural theology can unfortunately end up leading down the pathway to semi-deistic thinking. Michael Behe is an Associate Professor of Biochemistry at Lehigh University in the US who believes that biological diversity derives from common descent, but who is sceptical that the Darwinian processes of natural selection are sufficient to generate such complexity. Behe does not hold to Young Earth Creationism, but instead believes that there are "irreducibly complex systems" in cellular biochemistry that can only be explained by invoking a God of design. These systems, such as the clotting of blood and the molecular mechanisms involved in the immune system, only function correctly as complete systems and so Behe thinks that they could not have evolved gradually by Darwinian mechanisms.

Behe is a champion of what has come to be called the "Intelligent Design" (ID) movement, a way of thinking that purports to find direct evidence for God's actions based on scientific evidence. The theoretical underpinnings of the movement have been provided by a mathematician called William Dembski.[22] Dembski suggests that it is possible to infer that some systems, for example in biology, display what he calls "specified complexity." Such a designation can only be justified, Dembski claims, by first excluding the possibility that the system has been generated by what he calls "natural processes." Natural processes are presumed by Dembski to fall into one of three categories: chance, necessity or the joint action of chance and necessity. If it can be shown that the system or object in question could not possibly have been brought about by one of these three types of explanation, then they display "specified complexity" and must therefore be the products of "intelligent design."

A thorough critique of Dembski's thesis is outside the scope of this book.[23] Instead we shall briefly survey Behe's biologically based claims for ID within the scope of the "creation-evolution" debate and see if they stand up to closer scrutiny. There are at least two specific arenas in which, we think, Behe's arguments are weak: the scientific and the theological.

In the context of science Behe maintains that Darwinian mechanisms of natural selection are inadequate to explain the evolution of complex systems. He suggests that "irreducibly complex systems" such as blood-clotting mechanisms could not have come into being by such "chance" processes. Behe likens such systems, which require the cooperation of multiple proteins to have the desired end-effect, to a mousetrap, which only functions properly if all the components are put together simultaneously. How could such a system evolve gradually when each of the components taken separately would be of no particular use to the organism? Just as each separate component of the mousetrap would be of no use in catching mice, so each separate protein used in the blood-clotting process would be of no use without its interactions with all the others.

The problem for Behe's argument comes when you start looking more carefully at the genes that encode the proteins that are involved in blood clotting and also at simpler blood-clotting systems that are present in other animals. Blood clotting in most vertebrates like us is quite similar. It requires the presence of a fibrous, soluble protein called fibrinogen to circulate in our blood. Fibrinogen has a sticky center, but this region is normally kept well covered by the rest of the molecule. To form a clot a protease enzyme called thrombin cuts off the outside of the fibrinogen so that the sticky bits, now called fibrins, can stick together to start clot formation. Proteases are enzymes (proteins that act as catalysts) that clip bits off other proteins.

So why does thrombin suddenly start clipping bits off fibrinogen? The answer is that thrombin itself is activated by another protease called Factor X. And then in turn Factor X requires two more proteases, Factor VII and Factor IX, to switch it on, and they in turn need other factors. One of the essential factors is called Factor VIII which is defective in hemophiliacs, and who therefore suffer from faulty blood clotting. When Queen Victoria gave birth to her eighth child in 1853, assisted by the new anesthetic gas chloroform, little Prince Leopold turned out to be a "bleeder," and eventually died from a fall at the age of 31. This was the first indication that Queen Victoria was a carrier of hemophilia, and with time this mutant gene was spread through her descendants to many royal houses in Europe.

Altogether there are more than 20 components in the "reaction cascade" that results in clot formation. Why so many? The answer is that the cascade of steps whereby one protease activates another provides an amplification system in which an initial trigger can produce a very rapid response at the bottom of the cascade. So if a single active Factor (protease) can activate 20 molecules of the next Factor in the chain, and then that one activates 20 more, then a millionfold amplification of the initial signal can readily be achieved by such a system. And the trigger that makes the "clotting gun" fire is pulled by various factors released by damaged tissues that activate the first factor in the chain. Clotting would still occur without the amplification system, but it would just happen a lot more slowly.

Could a Darwinian mechanism explain how this system came into being? As it happens, quite easily. For a start it turns out that genes encoding proteases comprise as much as 2 percent of the whole human genome. Since we have about 30,000 genes, that means we have about 600 proteases. It is clear that many of these proteases have arisen by gene duplication. The proteases that comprise the cascade of factors involved in blood clotting are all related to each other—they are all members of the same protein "family."

The next part of the Darwinian explanation for the evolution of blood clotting requires that we should be able to find a gene encoding for fibrinogen in a simpler organism than vertebrates where it does a different job. We should also be able to find simpler blood clotting systems in the animals from which vertebrates evolved. Both of these requirements have been fulfilled. In 1990 a gene encoding a protein similar to fibrinogen was found in the sea cucumber, an echinoderm.[24] As far as simpler blood-clotting systems are concerned, it is intriguing to look at the systems that invertebrates use to prevent blood loss. Invertebrates such as star fish and worms don't bleed to death when they get a cut for two reasons: first, unlike us, their circulatory systems are under relatively low pressure; second, and of more relevance to the present argument, they have various forms of sticky white blood cells that are good at plugging leaks. So if a blood vessel is broken then white blood cells are swept into the hole where they become sticky, bind to other proteins like collagen, and block any further escape of blood. As a system it is not nearly as good as ours, but it is quite adequate for animals that don't have hearts pumping their blood around at high pressures.

So it is quite easy to envisage how the vertebrate clotting system may have evolved. Since fibrinogen-like molecules were already present, most likely in the blood plasma initially for other functions such as maintaining the correct osmotic pressure, all that was then necessary was for a protease such as thrombin to be mistargeted to the blood as a result of a mutation, a not unlikely scenario. Together with thrombin activation by a further protease this would then give a simple 3-component system that would be sufficient to cause blood clotting. This simple mechanism alone would have given the first vertebrates using it an immense selective advantage and the system would have therefore been passed on to many progeny. Other steps in the cascade may have been added later as incremental components, most likely due to gene duplication as discussed above, gradually building up to the multi-component, speedy system that is used in our bodies today.

So, far from being a "black box," blood-clotting mechanisms actually provide rather striking illustrations of the way in which multi-component systems can assemble by Darwinian mechanisms. The key point to remember is that such systems do not assemble all at once in a single organism (which really would be remarkable), but rather that each component is already present in order to carry out a different task altogether. There are many examples in biology of "moonlighting proteins"—proteins that carry out quite different tasks depending on whether they are inside the cell or outside, on the particular tissue in which they are located, or even which specific location they occupy inside a cell.[25] For example, there is one enzyme called phosphoglucose isomerase, which is a key enzyme in energy metabolism, but it also has at least four other quite different additional roles. This enzyme has probably been around in evolution for more than a billion years, because it is present in all the three major branches of life—the Eukaryotes (like us), the Eubacteria (microorganisms) and the Archaea (a domain of organisms that wasn't recognized until relatively recently). So it's had plenty of time to be used for other functions. By bringing two or three proteins together that already exist for other functions, then a simple system can be formed to do a specific job like blood clotting that gives the individual organism expressing that particular set of genes a big selective advantage. Later on in evolution further components can be added to the system incrementally to make it more sophisticated. Once a really efficient system is established in evolution, then organisms are naturally loathe to let it go. The vertebrate blood-clotting system has remained pretty stable now for the last 400 million years of evolution that separate us from the puffer fish.[26] If you have a good system on board, why change it?

We have examined Behe's blood-clotting example in some detail because if one of his examples in *Darwin's Black Box* fails to convince, then this tends to make the other examples proffered less plausible. And although we do not have space here to look at each example in detail, this is in fact the case. There are convincing Darwinian explanations for each of the supposedly "irreducibly complex" systems that Behe presents to us, not least the cilia that cells use to generate force and movement.[27] The immune system represents a further beautiful physiological system that only operates properly when all its various components are in place (involving hundreds of components, not 20 or so as with blood clotting). Yet our understanding of the evolution of the immune system has increased greatly over the past decade and we now know that many of the genes involved in our innate immune system are extremely old and may be found in organisms such as fruit flies (about 40 percent of our genes are shared with fruit flies and worms—enough to keep us humble!).

So the moral in science when it comes to present gaps in our knowledge is: "never say never." The history of science is littered with examples of people who thought that something would never be explained, or that something would never happen—and then it did, sometimes only a short while later. As Lord Kelvin pontificated in a speech to the British Association for the Advancement of Science around 1900, a few years before Einstein made his great discoveries: "There is nothing new to be discovered in physics now. All that remains is more and more precise measurement."

And it is this point that brings us to the key philosophical and theological weaknesses of Behe's thesis. For it is difficult to avoid the conclusion that Behe's argument is a somewhat updated version of the classic "god-of-the-gaps" argument for the existence of God. Behe points us to systems in biology for which he thinks science cannot provide adequate explanations, even in principle, and then suggests that those particular systems must be "designed," suggesting the existence of a supernatural designer.

But there are three fatal weaknesses in this line of thinking:

- If "design" can only refer to systems about which science is currently ignorant, then inevitably the design concept will shrink—and the designer as well—as the scientific explanations become more comprehensive. This is the classic problem with a god-of-the-gaps argument: "god" or the "designer" is used as an "explanation" to plug the current gap in our knowledge, but as our knowledge base grows, so the "god" shrinks.

- One invariably ends up in a muddle if metaphysical language and scientific descriptions are mingled together. More technically in philosophy this is called a "category error." "Design" is a word referring to purpose and intentionality. In human discourse it is common to refer to the "design" of a car engine, even though we have available to us a complete specification of how all the components of the engine operate to make the car move. We do not normally refer to things as being "designed" on the grounds that we do not have any explanation for how they came into being. Yet that is the use of the word "design" that Behe wishes us to make. And in the process he tries to invoke "design" as if it represents an explanation for something, when in reality it is just a rather unsatisfactory way of flagging up some gaps in our current scientific knowledge. As already noted, those gaps have a habit in any case of being filled rather rapidly.

- The situation becomes even more problematic when Behe suggests that, "If a biological structure can be explained in terms of those natural laws, then we cannot conclude that it was designed. . . . It turns out that the cell contains systems that span the range from obviously designed to no apparent design." As an example of biochemical structures that have not been designed Behe discusses cell membranes and hemoglobin. So Behe envisages the created order (although he does not call it that) as being divided into a non-designed aspect that works by natural laws and which science can currently describe, and a designed aspect that does not involve natural laws and which science cannot currently understand. It is in dissecting this argument that the semi-deism of Behe's position may be perceived most clearly. The key give-away phrase is where Behe states that, "Some features of the cell appear to be the result of simple natural processes, others probably so." Behe envisages a quasi-autonomous domain called "nature" in which there are "naturalistic processes" that science can explain, and a quite different domain in which the designer acts supernaturally to bring about designed processes that science is unable to explain.

The stance of robust theism toward the created order is very different from that proposed by the ID movement. Nature is "what God does." Therefore all scientific descriptions—without exception—represent descriptions of the creative and sustaining activities of God in the world around us. The properties of matter reflect God's creative power irrespective of whether or not we are currently in a position to understand them. Current gaps in our scientific knowledge should act as a spur and motivation for further research until we can make our scientific explanations more complete to the glory of God. Every component of cells, indeed every single entity described by biology, all equally represent the outworkings of God's activities in the created order.

In Christian theology there is no "two-tier" universe that one can split into the "designed" portion and the "undesigned" portion. As the psalmist wrote, the whole created order is such as to arouse our awe, wonder and worship,[28] but this is because every aspect of it, without exception, has God as its author.

We have dealt at some length with Behe's "Intelligent Design" approach because it illustrates rather well the way in which semi-deism can permeate even works that claim to be defending the Christian faith. One motivation appears to be the desire to underline the "miraculous" aspect of God's creative actions. If science cannot (currently) explain something very well, then this seems to provide scope for the miraculous. The problem with such an emphasis is that the Bible does not view God's creative actions as being miraculous. Instead the Bible repeatedly draws attention to the consistency of God's actions in creation. It is only because of this consistency that science is possible. Only if the material world behaves reproducibly is there the opportunity to carry out experiments and to formulate generalized laws describing the behavior of matter and energy.

The Bible sees the whole of creation as flowing out of God's word of command, and God goes on commanding his creation to continue until the present day, but the Bible does not describe this as "miraculous." Miracles are those special actions of God that play a key role in fulfilling God's salvation plan for humankind, but nearly always in the Bible they refer to signs of God's grace in particular human situations. Since the whole of creation derives from God's actions there is no notion that the created order per se is miraculous, in its origins any more than in its continued existence. This point was well understood by the writers of the Old Testament. For example, in Nehemiah Chapter 9 as the people of Israel are praying they give thanks to God for his creation (verse 6), but with no mention of miracles, and then a few moments later in the same prayer give thanks to God for his "miraculous signs and wonders" in delivering them out of Egypt.

The Medieval Church had a habit of proliferating miracles, no doubt in an attempt to impress the irreligious and to draw attention to the power of the Church. But one of the missions of the biblical reformers such as Calvin and Luther was to counteract this tendency, reminding their listeners of God's common grace, which was available to all. We should be careful that we do not repeat the error of the Medieval Church in calling some aspects of his creation miracles, which God himself has chosen not to call miracles in his biblical revelation to us.

CHAPTER 7

Genetics and Sex

Whereas evolution will hopefully fade away as a contentious issue, insofar as (some) atheists and (some) Christians stop investing it with unnecessary ideological significance, genetic engineering and novel reproductive technologies are likely to be continuing "hot issues" during the course of the twenty-first century. This is because the completion of the Human Genome Project, and continued advances in molecular genetics, will give us increased powers to manipulate our own DNA as well as the DNA of other animals and plants. At the same time our ability to manipulate cells in the laboratory for reproductive purposes continues at a great pace.

Genetic engineering

Imagine it is 20 years from now. By law it is now necessary to obtain your complete genome sequence at birth, which is then stored along with your other medical records. This will not only help predict the kinds of diseases that you might suffer from later in life, but will also be checked before you are given any medication to prevent unwanted side-effects. Your sequence will determine your life insurance premiums and will be used to check for any risk factors that might occur with your partner before having children.

Is that the kind of society we want?

The DNA of biology is very different from the DNA of popular culture, yet even stripped of its mystique it remains a remarkable molecule. Each of the 10^{28} somatic cells in our body contains 6 feet of DNA packaged with proteins to form 23 pairs of chromosomes. If all the DNA in all the cells in a single human being were stretched out it would reach to the moon and back 8,000 times! As millions of our cells divide every second, each individual produces thousands of miles every minute of newly copied DNA.

Human DNA contains around three thousand million nucleotides, the "letters" which comprise the genetic alphabet, encoding about 30,000 genes. There are only four "letters" in this alphabet. Each gene consists of a sequence of nucleotides which encodes a different protein. Only about 2 percent of human DNA encodes genes—some of the rest is involved in controlling how genes are switched on to make proteins, but the function of much of our DNA (if any) is not yet well understood. As we discussed in the previous chapter, the Human Genome Project has succeeded in obtaining our own complete DNA nucleotide sequence and the genome sequences of many other bacteria, animals and plants continue to be generated at a breathtaking pace. If the human DNA sequence were printed in books of 200 pages each, 5,000 books would be required. But already there is a company in the US that charges a mere $700,000 for you to buy your child's genome sequence and the same company already envisages bringing that cost down to $1,000 in future years.

The DNA sequences of different individuals (except identical twins) vary to such an extent that everyone alive today is different, not only from everyone else, but from everyone who has ever lived or ever will live. On average, two people differ in about one DNA letter per 1,300, or about 2.3 million nucleotides in total, due to naturally occurring mutations—if this were not the case then we would all look identical! DNA is not a static molecule but is in a state of flux. Fortunately this flux is not very fast, otherwise we would not be here to discuss it.

The genetic code is essentially identical for all living organisms from bacteria, yeast and viruses to dandelions, kangaroos and humans. This is the most powerful argument for the unity of all living things and is what makes genetic engineering possible. Genetic engineering refers to the techniques whereby recombinant DNA, hybrid DNA made by artificially joining pieces of DNA from different sources, is produced and utilized.

All the "tools" of the genetic engineer are natural products, such as the various enzymes that act like scissors to cut the DNA at precise points and then paste the pieces together again. Recombinant DNA by itself can do nothing unless it is incorporated into a cell to make a protein. To do this the DNA is packaged into a carrier, normally a plasmid (a small circle of DNA that can transfer genes) or a virus, disabled so that it cannot damage the host cell. Thus, genetic engineering mimics processes already occurring in the natural world in which DNA is transferred into new cellular locations.

There is no doubt that genetic engineering, as with any other technology, has great potential for misuse. Humanistic science has not been immune from arrogance in its utopian ambitions. The history of the eugenics movement provides many unfortunate examples of such human folly. In the early twentieth century, for example, 30 states in the US enacted eugenic laws that included directives for compulsory sterilization for those considered to be "feeble-minded" or "hereditary defectives." A total of over 60,000 Americans were eventually to suffer involuntary sterilization under these laws, reaching a peak in the 1920s and 1930s.[1] At the time, the eugenics research was considered to be "scientific," although the vast majority of it has since been completely discredited. It is therefore vital that the debate about genetic engineering remains firmly in the public domain, and that the public in general remain active and well-informed in their contributions.

Christians in particular are already very involved in genetic engineering and in its applications to feed a hungry world and to detect and (ultimately) cure human diseases. The fact that the Human Genome Project itself has been coordinated by a committed Christian, Francis Collins, provides just one example out of many that could be cited. "I find no discordance," writes Collins, "between being a scientist who insists on absolute rigor in studying the natural world and being a person of faith who believes in a personal God. In that context, I find those rare dramatic moments of scientific discovery in my own experience to be moments of worship also, where a revelation about some new intricacy of God's creation is appreciated for the first time."[2] Collins also makes the vital comment that "Good theology needs accurate science." As with the debate about evolution, Christians have sometimes been guilty of sloppy thinking when making public pronouncements about genetic engineering. A thorough understanding of what it involves is essential if a sensible debate is to ensue.

Genetic engineering is routinely used in research in thousands of laboratories worldwide. Most manipulations are carried out on cell lines or bacteria, applications which have raised little ethical controversy. In the human context the way in which the media has handled the issue of genetic engineering has often been alarmist and sensationalist, deflecting attention from that small proportion of situations in which the new technology does raise serious and immediate ethical issues.

Biblical perspectives on genetic engineering

The Bible gives some important principles that can be used when thinking through the applications of genetic engineering.

- The Bible's robust theism that we have already emphasized implies that the DNA which underlies all biological diversity is as much the product of God's authorship[3] as any other of creation's myriad aspects. DNA in God's world is no icon but represents just one more example of God's creative handiwork, demythologized of any mystique that popular culture might wish to bestow.

- Human beings are "made in God's image"[4] and therefore have a special value independent of the genetic variation that exists between them. The value and special status of humans is reflected in the weighty responsibility that God has given us to care for creation using our God-given gifts to explore the world.[5] The fact that God loves and cares for each human individual irrespective of their genetic endowment provides a solid rationale for their value. Even though they may not always be able to fulfil, at least in this life, all their potential as stewards of God's creation, nevertheless the solidarity of the human community with them should be apparent. It should be noted that whereas such aspirations are shared with many who ascribe to no particular religious beliefs, nevertheless it is within the Christian framework that the absolute value of the individual is rationally guaranteed due to the creational relationship between God and humankind.

- The biblical doctrine of the Fall—the entry of sin into the world—reminds us of how far the world is from what God intended. It has ensured that human earth-keeping will never be fully as God intended, at least not in this "present evil age."[6] The exploration of God's created order for the good of humankind is one of the joys and privileges of being a scientist, but Christians are acutely aware that human knowledge tarnished with sin can be used for evil purposes. Christians will therefore be suspicious of arrogant or naively optimistic attitudes toward the exploitation of the natural world, not least its DNA.

- The biblical doctrine of redemption—the restoration of estranged human beings to God—reminds us that God's plan is not only for the salvation of individuals, but encompasses the whole created order. In his letter written to the early church in Rome, the apostle Paul writes of a creation that has "been groaning as in the pains of childbirth" waiting "in eager expectation for the sons of God to be revealed."[7] In the context of the passage the term "sons of God" refers to Christians, those who have entered into God's family by new birth. So Paul is saying that "the sons of God," God's new family, are redeemed to becoming the kind of earth-keepers that God intended. As God's people join in God's work of liberating creation from its bondage to decay, so they act as a signpost pointing forward to the new earth, which God is one day going to bring into being.[8] Earth-keeping in the present is only a pilot-project compared with the full redemption that God promises in his new earth, but it is that full redemption in the future that gives to the present both its rationale and its hope.

Some objections to genetic engineering

It is sometimes objected that genetic engineering is "unnatural." Ironically, in marked contrast to other recent technologies, the "toolkit" of the genetic engineer is entirely derived from products found naturally within the created order. What people mean by "natural" often turns out to mean "what I personally am used to." Flying, watching TV and car driving all appeared unnatural at first. Furthermore, "naturalness" does not necessitate desirability. Pathogenic viruses, bacteria and mosquitoes are all natural, but people generally approve of destroying them whenever possible. "Naturalness" is therefore of doubtful relevance to the ethical debate about genetic engineering.

A more substantial argument suggests that we should not change the inviolable *ousia* (essence) or *telos* (goal) of any living organism. Both concepts come directly from Aristotelian philosophy. The genetic engineering of female turkeys to make them less broody (so that they lay more eggs) has been attacked by Jeremy Rifkin as "a serious violation of the intrinsic value of the creature."[9] The precise definition of this "essence" or "goal" is, however, problematic. The domestication of animals and the breeding of new crop strains for food have been going on for many millennia. Is the "essence" of a species supposed to refer to its original state or its present state? Is the "essence" of dog-hood better represented by a Pekinese or by a Great Dane? Both belong to the same species. If "essence" is taken to refer to the genome of a plant or animal as if it were a static entity, then this is simply false. DNA is always changing, albeit slowly. In practice the applications of genetic engineering are not to change the identity of species but to introduce minor genetic modifications into plants and animals to make them more productive in farming or, as discussed below, to prevent and cure human disease.

Another favourite phrase used by some is that genetic engineering involves "playing god." The term *hubris* was used in Greek philosophy to refer to the supposed impiety involved in delving into the realms of the gods.[10] Similar ideas are apparent in some contemporary ecological thinking that views nature as sacred and therefore inviolable. However, the biblical doctrine of creation has demythologized nature of these semi-divine overtones and given humankind a specific mandate to care for the earth and its biological diversity,[11] a mandate that if anything was made even more explicit after the Fall.[12] We are called not to "play God" but to be responsible stewards of all that God has given us. As Donald MacKay has written: "In place of the craven fear instilled by a pagan theology of nature . . . the Christian who finds scientific talents in his toolbag has quite a different fear—the fear that his Father should judge him guilty of neglecting his stewardly responsibilities by failing to pursue the opportunities for good that may be opened up by the new developments."[13] Christians should approach such responsibilities not with the arrogance implicit in the phrase "playing God," but with prayerful concern that we should be responsible earth-keepers under God.

Genetically modified foods

The applications of genetic engineering to farming provide good examples of what such stewardship can involve. About one-third to one-half of all agricultural production worldwide is lost to pests and diseases and there is enormous scope for genetic engineering to render crops resistant to pests, drought and frost, to improve yields and to enable food to be produced in harsh environments. The central Christian concern will be to utilize the new technology to feed a hungry world and to distribute its benefits more equitably.

A GM crop plant is one that contains at least one transgene, from another plant of the same species or from a completely different species, inserted artificially instead of through pollination.[14] Most of those developed or proposed confer resistance to a herbicide, to an insect (e.g., genetically modified to express the insect toxin *Bacillus thuringensis*) or to a plant viral pathogen. Other desirable traits conferred include salt or drought tolerance, and improved storage characteristics. Currently, the area planted with GM crops worldwide is 53 million hectares, mainly in the US, Argentina, Canada, China and Australia. Five million farmers, of whom three quarters are smallholders in China, are growing GM crops. In North America, GM crops have been grown for some years, the US area having increased about twentyfold between 1996 and 2003. More than half of the world's soybean is now GM herbicide-tolerant. Other major GM crops currently grown are: corn and cotton, canola (elsewhere termed "rapeseed oil"), and GM virus-resistant potato, squash and papaya.

European countries have generally been more cautious about the introduction of GM crops in relation to the rest of the world. Since there are already food mountains in the high-income parts of the world, the pressure to produce food more efficiently is likely to be of commercial benefit to the producer rather than the consumer. Nevertheless there are significant benefits for the environment in utilizing pest-resistant crop strains that make frequent chemical treatment of crops unnecessary. For example, the use of pesticide-resistant cotton has resulted in 1.2 million kg less pesticide being applied, an 80 percent reduction in usage in China, and a subsequent increase in non-target insects.[15] Extensive testing on a case-by-case basis prior to general commercial use seems a sensible approach.

The Bible is insistent in its reminders that we should have a particular concern for the poor[16] and in distributing benefits equitably,[17] so the Christian's interests in providing GM foods for the world will be particularly influenced by these emphases. In this respect, developments by subsistence farmers to use GM crops are encouraging. In the tropics the publicly funded Consultative Group on International Agricultural Research (CGIAR) institutes all have plant-breeding programs devoted to Third World applications which include GM.[18] Some tropical parasitic weeds, such as *Striga* and *Orobanche,* are so pernicious that they can completely destroy the crop of subsistence farmers. Over 1,000 biotechnologists are working in laboratories throughout Asia, mainly on GM rice varieties. By 2000 there were over 10,000 field trials in 39 countries. In one detailed study, 395 small-scale low-income farmers who grew pest-resistant GM cotton in seven different Indian states found that the technology reduced damage by pests and increased yields by an average 80 percent.[19] This contrasts with a yield advantage of less than 10 percent on average for comparable crops grown in the US and China. The Indian study showed that insecticide use was reduced on average by almost 70 percent.

Of course GM foods are not by any means the only solution for the agricultural needs of low-income countries. Effective distribution of foods already available, better use of appropriate local technologies, and the resolution of political conflict, are all essential components in a complex patchwork of economic solutions. But those who express hostility to GM foods should nevertheless reflect on the likely implications of their actions for feeding hungry people. In 1997–99 (the most recent figures available at the time of writing) there were 815 million undernourished people in the world.[20] Since the mid-1960s there has been a dramatic cut in the number of undernourished people, largely due to huge reductions in poverty in China. Remove China from the picture and the number of undernourished people in the other low-income countries actually increased by more than 40 million due to the massive overall increase in world population. World population is now 6 billion and is projected to grow to 8.3 billion by 2030. Such an increase would require a 40–45 percent increase in food production, so the potential scope for GM technologies in preventing worldwide hunger is significant.

Screening for defective genes in medicine

Besides GM foods, the arena for genetic engineering that has aroused most controversy and ethical heart-searching is in its medical applications. The central concern in this context is the detection and cure of genetically inherited diseases, of which about 5,000 are known. Probably we all carry at least one lethal gene, but fortunately most of our genes come in pairs and usually both members of the pair have to be defective for a disease to develop.

The earliest immediate practical application of the Human Genome Project is likely to be an increase in the number of tests available for *screening defective genes*. Mass screening has usually been counterproductive, unless a particular population has a very high prevalence of a defective gene. More usually, screening is carried out in families where a risk of genetic disease is already established. Different ethical issues are raised depending on whether screening is prenatal or postnatal.

Prenatal screening of fetuses may be associated with abortion, a thorny topic about which Christians have disagreements. Prenatal screening per se does not depend on genetic engineering and has been carried out since the 1970s. Typically it is offered to a pregnant mother in cases where both parents are known to be heterozygous ("carriers") for a specific lethal genetic disease. This means that any child born in that family has a 1 in 4 chance of being affected by that disease. Tests are carried out using a tiny sample of cells obtained from the fetus. If the fetus is found to carry the disease, then the pregnancy may be terminated. Such terminations comprise less than 3 percent of the approximately 1.3 million abortions performed annually in the US. Some Christians are strongly against a liberal policy on abortion and yet believe that termination of pregnancy is preferable to giving birth to a child who, in many cases, will appear normal at birth, but who is then certain to die a slow and painful death within the first decade of life. Such is the outcome, for example, of most lysosomal storage diseases. In contrast to such 100 percent certainties, one effect of using DNA tests for prenatal diagnosis will be to increase the number of cases in which percentage risk factors of developing a disease in later life can be estimated. It is this latter class of information that is most fraught with ethical dilemmas. Similar dilemmas are already raised by the availability of prenatal diagnosis for the chromosomal abnormality which leads to Down's Syndrome, a condition with unpredictable effects ranging from mild to severe abnormality.

It should be noted at this juncture that the techniques developed by scientists to carry out prenatal diagnoses are not really ethically neutral. The scientist might argue that the technology generated is neutral, and only its application raises ethical issues, but in practice this is disingenuous. Without the availability of the technology there would be no decision to make and no possibility of aborting an affected fetus for such a reason. We mention this not as a general criticism of prenatal diagnosis, but to illustrate the way in which moral issues are integral to certain types of scientific research.

One way of avoiding yet more abortions is by the use of preimplantation genetic diagnosis (PGD). As with other forms of prenatal diagnosis, this procedure is usually carried out when both parents are known carriers of a lethal disease. Preimplantation genetic diagnosis involves in vitro fertilization followed by growth of the embryo to the stage at which it contains 4–8 cells. One or two cells can then be removed without damaging the embryo and defective genes identified. Clearly defective embryos are discarded and only the healthy embryo is implanted in the mother. To date, PGD has been most widely used to prevent the birth of children with chromosomal disorders such as Down's Syndrome, or with genetic disorders due to specific gene defects, such as Tay-Sachs disease, cystic fibrosis, sickle cell disease, Huntington's Chorea, and Cooley's anemia. With the current available technology, the PGD laboratory cannot truly screen for multiple possible abnormalities. It can only identify the presence or absence of a specific disorder. Only a few thousand preimplantation genetic diagnoses have been carried out so far worldwide, and in the USA the technique is only offered by a few specialised centers, but use of the technique is likely to increase markedly as more DNA tests become available. The procedure has the great advantage that it avoids the need for aborting an affected foetus post-implantation, as required by current prenatal diagnostic procedures, although it remains technically demanding and expensive. In assessing the ethical implications involved, it should be kept in mind that about

80 percent of all embryos fail to implant following in vitro fertilization or natural fertilization. Some of these embryos demonstrate severe chromosomal abnormalities, apparently "nature's way" of preventing the birth of children carrying genetic defects. It could therefore be argued that in preimplantation genetic diagnosis, human intervention is merely extending this natural process of viable embryo selection.

It is apparent that PGD has the potential for abuse. Indeed it is not allowed in many countries (e.g., Germany, Austria, Switzerland, Argentina). In the United Kingdom it is a procedure regulated by license from the Human Fertilisation and Embryology Authority (HFEA) under the terms of the Human Fertilisation and Embryology Act (1990). The central aim of the procedure as enshrined in current UK regulations is to prevent the birth of children affected with life-threatening genetic disorders. The use of PGD for sex determination outside this aim is forbidden by the HFEA. As with any new medical technology there is also a gray area in which ethical decisions are particularly controversial. This was highlighted by the use of PGD to ensure the birth of a baby boy "tissue-typed" so that he could become a donor of haematopoietic stem cells for his sister who suffered from Fanconi's anemia.[21] In this case PGD was used solely for the purpose of tissue-typing. In this country the HFEA is now allowing tissue-typing only in those cases where PGD is in any case being carried out on a pre-implantation embryo for a life-threatening disease. The direction such selection procedures might potentially take is illustrated by a case in the US in which a child was deliberately conceived using donor insemination by a male with a genetic history of deafness, to be deaf like its lesbian parents.[22] Ethically it seems wise to focus the use of PGD on the prevention of babies carrying lethally destructive genetic mutations and to avoid using the procedure for generating children for utilitarian purposes that might be judged beneficial to their parents or their siblings, but which carry no conceivable benefit to their own welfare. In a market-driven society the commodification of babies is a real danger and the intrinsic value of each human individual irrespective of their genetic endowment needs persistent emphasis.

Likewise the use of PGD for the pre-implantation selection of embryos on the basis of trivial genetic characteristics without medical implications should be avoided. The emotive term "designer baby" so loved by the media in such discussions is inaccurate as the key human action involved is one of embryo selection not of design. Nevertheless, public unease over excessive levels of selection and control over another person's life are well-founded. Christians who believe that the use of PGD is an ethically justified use of technology should also be supportive of the

HFEA's present stance to keep this form of pre-implantation genetic diagnosis only for severe and life-threatening conditions.

Further technical developments may eventually make the need for PGD redundant. There are active research programs in various countries to develop ways of producing and growing both sperm and eggs in the laboratory.[23] Eventually it may prove possible to screen both sperm and eggs for genetic abnormalities in the laboratory prior to in vitro fertilization, followed by implantation of a healthy embryo into the mother. Although such procedures are many years away, they will remove some of the ethical concerns about present prenatal screening approaches.

Postnatal screening raises rather different issues. Where prevention or treatment of diseases is possible, there seems every reason to proceed. Every baby born in the US, as in many other countries, undergoes mandatory screening for the genetic disease phenylketonuria. If untreated, this disease results in severe mental retardation, but, once detected, is easily prevented by minor dietary adjustments. This is a good example of a genetic outcome being radically altered by a small change of environment. Knowing that defective genes are present can enable affected individuals to change their diet and lifestyle in an attempt to counteract their effects. Those who carry the *BRCA-1* or *BRCA-2* gene mutations that increase the risk of breast cancer can, at least, go for more frequent check-ups as early diagnosis and intervention is the key to treating such cancers.

Where no treatment is available, different issues arise.[24] Receiving general information about the genetic basis for human disease is very different from the momentous implications of hearing that *you* personally carry a defective gene. For example, Huntington's disease develops in people aged 40 to 50 and there is at present no cure. After some years of increasing loss of motor control, death occurs 10–15 years after the first onset of symptoms. A DNA test can now tell a person at risk that they carry the defective gene. A knee-jerk reaction might conclude that such information is too heavy a load for anyone to bear. However, knowledge that one is carrying a lethal gene might enable a choice to be made as to whether to have children and whether to pursue a different career. With professional counselling and support, the prospect of future suffering might accentuate the need to use the years of health to the best advantage. It is surely far better to have a fruitful short life than a fruitless long one, Jesus himself providing us with the perfect example.

As postnatal screening becomes more widespread, two urgent ethical issues require continued attention. First, screening may lead to people having information about their lives about which they can do nothing. Such information may increase stress and may also be misused by others if confidentiality is breached. The right *not* to know one's genetic heritage is as important, perhaps more important, than the right to know. Such issues can be particularly pressing as companies increasingly promote home testing, or the sending of samples from home to be tested elsewhere.[25] At first sight this may seem a bit like pregnancy testing where a test can be carried out quickly and easily with a home-kit. But the implications of genetic testing are very different. For a start, most of the common diseases that afflict people in the high-income countries, such as heart disease and cancer, are multigenic in nature—in other words the conditions are influenced by a complex array of genetic factors and, in any case, environmental factors such as diet and lifestyle often remain more important than genetic factors. Even in those few cases where a single gene defect is a direct predictor of disease in later life (as with Huntington's disease), it is highly unwise to embark on such testing without adequate explanation and counselling regarding its implications. If you find that you are a carrier of some deadly disease, then this has implications for all your blood relatives who may be carriers as well. So testing should never be undertaken lightly and is best carried out following advice from a professional medical practitioner.

Second, screening may create an underclass of carriers of deleterious genes who will become increasingly marginalized from the benefits of society, for example, by being unable to obtain mortgages or life insurance. Christians, however, along with many others, will view all people as having equal value irrespective of their genetic inheritance and will press for insurance practices that allow the equitable pooling of risk.[26]

Genetic therapies

Generally when people hear about the potential applications of genetic engineering to medicine, they immediately start thinking about the scope for genetically modifying people, a good dose of science-fiction films helping to shift their imagination into realms still far from medical reality. There are in principle two types of genetic therapies: those in which defective genes are replaced and those in which the goal is to add additional qualities to the individual that lie beyond the normal range of genetic variation currently found within human populations.

Replacement therapies could, in principle, be carried out in either somatic or in germ-line cells. Somatic cells are all those cells of the body that are not involved in reproduction. Somatic cell replacement thera-pies have already been used since 1990 with limited success as an experi-mental approach for treating several genetic diseases. Ethically, such procedures are no different from other novel medical technologies and carry the same kind of risk.

In 2002 the applications of genetic engineering in the somatic cell therapy of genetic disease at last began to yield some positive results, al-beit modest and not without setbacks. In April of that year, following a gene therapy trial that occurred two years previously, French researchers announced that the immune systems of several children with X-linked severe combined immunodeficiency (SCID) were nearly normal. Out of the 11 children in the trial at the Necker Hospital in Paris, 9 were cured. A successful and improved gene-transfer protocol for treating SCID pa-tients with adenosine deaminase deficiency was also reported at about the same time. Unfortunately, however, two of the Necker Hospital SCID patients later developed a leukemia-like condition.[27] The potential risk of such "insertional mutagenesis" events remains a matter for active discussion and is likely to impinge on the 600 gene therapy trials already ongoing worldwide.

Eventually it is likely that safe and successful genetic therapies will be found for a wide range of genetic diseases. But the pathway to success is likely to be littered with disappointments, and it is therefore important that the hopes of patients for instant cures are not raised prematurely.

In contrast to somatic cell therapies, all germ-cell replacement therapies are currently proscribed and are technically hazardous at pres-ent. In principle the therapy could involve, for example, in vitro fertiliza-tion for parents who are known carriers of lethal genes, followed by genetic surgery of a defective 4–8-cell embryo. In practice, however, there would be little point in carrying out such a procedure, since PGD would be available. In theory it might seem more acceptable ethically to heal the defective embryo. In practice, however, Christians who take an "absolutist" view of the value of such early embryos should realize that their stance may encourage development of the DNA technology for manipulation of human germ-line cells, which could increase social pressure for the use of additive therapies. A futuristic alternative is the screening of sperm and eggs for defective genes prior to fertilization, followed by in vitro fertilization using only healthy gametes.

Additive therapies, whether at the somatic cell or germ-line cell level, are currently technically impossible and are proscribed in the United Kingdom and the United States, as in other countries. The aim of such procedures would be to add to the individual person specific quali-ties not already encoded by their genome. Additive therapies therefore represent a radically different set of goals from those that aim to prevent or to cure human disease. Fortunately the human genome is immensely complex and numerous genes interact to generate human capacities in ways that we understand but dimly. There is no single gene "for" intelligence, or "for" musical ability or "for" homosexuality. In fact the question of whether there is any genetic contribution at all to these and many other facets of human behavior remains hotly disputed. The complexity of the human genome remains its best protection against those who might wish to add extra information content, for the simple reason that the effects of manipulating human DNA in such a way would be very likely to have quite unpredictable consequences on the functioning of other genes. Whereas it may be justified to take medical risks, or administer novel drugs, when making heroic efforts to save a patient's life who is at death's door, this is irrelevant to "additive therapies." Since experimenting with human beings is unethical, the risk argument alone provides a strong argument against additive therapies.

But for the Christian there is an even more important argument, namely, the fact that we are now, with our current genetic endowment, made "in the image of God," so defining clear boundaries. Accepting the term "image of God" to refer to all those qualities that characterize humans in their God-given tasks of being his delegated "earth-keepers," in particular our spiritual capacity for fellowship with God, the dangers of trying to add to what God has given us become apparent. The builders of the Tower of Babel[28] thought that their improved technology would allow them to reach up to heaven using their own human wisdom, but the result was confusion. The biblical record, not to speak of subsequent human history, makes it clear that human pretensions to self-grandeur invariably end in disaster. It is vital that we do not misuse God's good gift of genetic engineering to repeat such mistakes.

Overall, therefore, Christians should view the applications of genetic engineering as part of their overall concern and care for the environment, as the next chapter discusses further. Wise stewardship of DNA is as relevant as caring for other aspects of the earth's diversity. On some of the fine ethical detail, Christians may well disagree about the varied applications of genetic engineering. The issues are often complex and crystal clear answers are not always available. Christians will also often find themselves campaigning with "co-belligerents" in society whose religious or philosophical positions are markedly different from their own, yet whose stance on genetic engineering demonstrates similar ethical concerns. Having said that, it is striking that the Christian worldview par excellence provides a framework in which all people are of equal value irrespective of race, color or genetic endowment. God's unconditional love for each human individual provides a solid foundation for their absolute value, providing a powerful platform for defending the rights of those whose genetic endowment may be less fortunate than our own, and a strong motivation for healing genetic disease as this becomes increasingly technically feasible.

The cloning debate[29]

The fog on the M4 was exceptionally dense as the Robinson family drove toward London on 20 November 2011. Their only child Susan, aged 4, was playing happily with her dolls on the back seat. After years of unsuccessfully trying for a baby the Robinsons had eventually decided to use in vitro fertilization to have Susan, so she was especially cherished. Her long eyelashes and dimples were the spitting image of her mum, whereas even at that young age her long limbs held great promise of future athletic prowess, or so her proud father liked to think.

Suddenly a pile-up loomed out of the fog in front of them. Mr Robinson slammed on the brakes. His quick responses prevented their car diving into the mangled heap of wrecked cars ahead, but unfortunately the lorry driver behind was not so alert, sliding into their rear with a sickening thud. Seconds later the shocked parents found themselves clutching Susan's lifeless form as they huddled on the embankment, waiting for help to arrive.

Minutes later, after a short but fevered discussion, Mrs Robinson called CLON777 on her mobile and as the fog began to clear a helicopter landed in a nearby field, CLONE-AID emblazoned across its fuselage. A white-coated medical technician leapt from the helicopter and was soon taking tiny skin samples from Susan's limp body. Minutes later the samples were being stimulated in a nearby CLONE-AID laboratory to establish cell cultures.

Several months went by whilst the Robinsons grieved for little Susan, but finally they could contain themselves no longer. They wanted a replacement Susan and they wanted her now. Fortunately Mrs Robinson already had viable eggs frozen down as a result of her cycle of in vitro fertilization. The great day came. In the CLONE-AID laboratory, with its picture of Dolly the sheep proudly displayed on the wall, the process of "nucleus transfer" began (see figure for a description of how cloning can be carried out). A nucleus was removed from one of Susan's cultured skin cells. This single nucleus contained the cell's DNA with its genetic instructions to build a new Susan. Carefully the nucleus was placed in a small dish with one of Mrs Robinson's eggs from which the nucleus had been removed. A small electric current was zapped through the cell suspension and the nucleus fused with the egg cell to produce a tiny embryo. This procedure was repeated several times to generate several embryos that were carefully screened over the next few days to check for any abnormalities before one of them was implanted in Mrs Robinson. Nine months later the Robinsons held in their arms a pink and gorgeous looking "replacement Susan," complete with dimples, prominent eyelashes and long limbs.

Science fiction? At the moment, yes, as well as illegal, at least in the US as in many other countries. In 1998, 2001 and 2003 the US House of Representatives voted to ban all forms of human cloning, both reproductive and therapeutic. Some states in addition ban the use of stem cell therapies, while some others outlaw only reproductive cloning. It is a criminal offense to place in a woman an embryo created by any means other than fertilization. But it is not impossible that reproductive cloning will be attempted somewhere in the world. Even now various maverick doctors are claiming that they have already "treated" several infertile women who are pregnant with cloned babies. Whether this is a publicity stunt or true, only time will tell. But, fact or fantasy, it is unlikely that the issue of reproductive human cloning will go away.

WHY CLONE?

Why on earth would someone wish to clone themselves? All kinds of reasons have been proposed: as a last-ditch attempt to overcome infertility; to generate a "replacement child," like Susan; to create a child with perfectly matched tissues for possible transplant to a sick sibling; to enable homosexual couples to have children sharing the genes of one of them; out of curiosity; as part of cultic practices—and so the list could go on.

The theological and ethical issues involved are quite distinct from those relating to so-called "therapeutic cloning." This procedure, made legal in the United Kingdom in 2001, aims to use stem cells from early embryos for medical therapies. The main ethical issue surrounds the use of early human embryos as a source of stem cells, and we will discuss therapeutic cloning separately below.

SAFETY ISSUES

One of the main reasons that reproductive cloning remains illegal and is opposed by the great majority of people within the medical and scientific communities, is because of safety issues.

How to clone a sheep (or a human?)

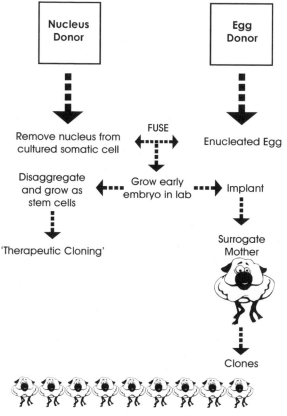

- Fetuses produced by nuclear transfer are ten times more likely to die in utero than fetuses produced by normal sexual means, while cloned offspring are three times more likely to die soon after birth. Cloning humans would always remain experimental, with risks of high fetal loss and deformities in the newborn. This point is particularly potent because the method used to create Dolly does not appear to work in primates, in contrast to mice, cattle and horses.[30]

- All somatic cells (namely, all our cells except the germ-line sperm and egg cells) accumulate mutations in their DNA during the course of life. These are not passed on to offspring during normal mating and are usually harmless. However, if several mutations accumulate in the same cell, then the cell may become cancerous. In nuclear transfer the nucleus from a random somatic cell is used in which the DNA will already have accumulated unknown mutations. These could lead to cancer in the clone.

- Genomic imprinting represents a further risk factor. Although genes encoding the same proteins are present in duplicate on paired chromosomes in somatic cells, in genomic imprinting one copy of a gene is switched off, depending on whether it came from the father or mother. Cloning also requires that the gene expression of a somatic donor nucleus has to be returned to an embryonic pattern of expression. In nuclear transfer the normal imprinting process may be disrupted, leading to abnormalities in development.

- Dolly was created by nuclear transfer from the mammary gland of a 6-year-old ewe and her cells already showed signs of aging soon after birth. Aging cloned mice become obese, die prematurely and have tumors.[31] Premature aging of a human clone is a real risk factor.

As Ian Wilmut, leader of the team that cloned Dolly, warns: "How can all the potential hazards be identified and quantified so that we know in advance what the risks would be if anyone did attempt to clone a human being? They can't."[32] Human cloning will always represent an experiment and experimenting on children is wrong. There are times when human curiosity should for ever remain unsatisfied.

CLONING, DETERMINISM AND HUMAN IDENTITY

There are some common misconceptions about human cloning. For example, some of the suggested reasons for cloning are based on a false premise: it is not the case that genetic identity implies identity of personality, talent or biography. Human development is shaped by a complex and continuous interplay between the individual and their environment. Identical twins are notable for their differences as well as for their similarities. Clones would be even more different than twins because they would not share the same womb and they would be born at different times. The grieving parents who seek to replace their dead child by cloning will be disappointed, for the clone will have a different personality, different gifts and interests, and a different biography. Each child is unique and irreplaceable. The parents would double their suffering by the tragedy of unfulfilled expectations and the clone might live under the terrible burden of knowing that they could never live up to those expectations.

The desire to replicate exceptional human talent would probably be similarly disappointed. There is no convincing evidence that complex human behaviors of any kind are inherited. Hitler's clone might decide to become an Austrian bus-driver. The brilliant novelist might turn out to be more interested in stamp collecting. Genetic determinism is a myth.

Nevertheless, on the other side of the coin, physical beauty (or lack of it) and athletic potential are to a large degree inherited. Many diseases also have a genetic component. The clone might experience a deep sense of genetic fatalism as they observe the medical history of the nucleus-donor, assuming that the clone knows the identity of this individual.

CLONING AND THE IMAGE OF GOD

What if all the technical problems were ironed out and sometime in the future cloning became even safer than a normal birth? Arguably this will never happen for the reasons given above. But it makes a good thought experiment, for it forces us to think through the issue: "Does Christian theology have anything distinctive to say about cloning?" We think it does, particularly when we consider biblical teaching in the light of insights provided by psychology and sociology.

The biblical teaching that is most relevant to the cloning debate concerns the "image of God." Many commentators have drawn attention to the "relational" perspective that is implicit in the biblical passages that refer to the "image of God" and, arguably, it is this emphasis which is most relevant in the cloning debate. There are only three passages in the Old Testament that provide explicit teaching about the "image of God" (Genesis 1:26–28; 5:1–5; 9:1–7), whereas the theme is more common in the New Testament, particularly in the context of the restoration of the image, spoilt by sin, through Christ's redemptive work.

The reflection of God's character on earth begins with a strong hint at God's own relational character: "Let us make man in our image . . ." (Genesis 1:26), an allusion greatly expanded in the trinitarian theology of the New Testament. God has been Father, Son and Holy Spirit for all eternity, a being in everlasting personal relationship, and as God creates humankind in God's image, so God likewise creates beings intended to be in relationship both with God and with each other. Furthermore, in trinitarian theology persons are defined by being related to another who is *different:* individual distinction rests on an asymmetric mutuality in which Father and Son are not mirror images (asymmetry), but neither can the Father be the Father unless he has a Son (mutuality).

It is striking that the Genesis "image of God" passages refer in each case to the relationship between God and Adam in the sense of humankind, explicitly referring in each case to the diversity of God's creation in making male and female.[33] The love that exists between Father, Son and Holy Spirit is to be reflected not by the atomized selves—so characteristic of western individualism—but in the love displayed in human relationships. The faithful reflection of God's image by male and female is unambiguously presented as sexual union leading to procreation: *Adam* was to be fruitful and increase in number (Genesis 1:28); *Adam* was created male and female (Genesis 5:1–2), a comment followed by an exposition of fruitfulness (Genesis 5:3–32); significantly, fruitful procreation still remains the mandate in humankind's post-Fall state (Genesis 9:6–7). The creation ordinance of sexual union within the boundaries of a loving, committed, marriage relationship is continuously emphasized throughout the Bible. When the New Testament searches for language that will do justice to the profound implications of becoming one flesh within the context of marriage (Genesis 2:24), it is the relationship between Christ and his Church that provides the striking analogy (Ephesians 5:22–33). God could have made us to reproduce asexually, as many species do, but in fact God made us as relational sexual beings.[34]

CLONING AND SOCIAL DISCOMBOBULATION

The application of biblical teaching on the "image of God" becomes apparent as soon as we start considering the likely impact on social and familial structures in the event that cloning ever became a dominant method for procreation. Families are God's ordained way of structuring society so that sexual union is linked to procreation within the solid bonds of a marriage partnership—and so that children are reared, protected, disciplined and educated within a loving and stable environment. Extensive reproductive cloning would profoundly disrupt the social structure of the family, and therefore of society. Procreation in the context of a loving relationship would be replaced by a sexless reproductive technique for which neither love nor a relationship is necessary.

The fact that genetic and personal identities are distinct does not imply that biological relationships have no bearing at all on human interactions. The evidence suggests otherwise. People who have never known their biological parents have a powerful drive to discover and meet them—the theme of numerous books and films. Cloning would divorce genetic parenthood from relational parenthood. The biological parent of the clone would not be the nucleus-donor, but the parents of the donor. The genetic parents of the clone would therefore be the grandparents in generational terms. If the clone was reproduced in turn to populate the next generation, then the biological parents would now be the great-grandparents, and if cloning were continued the parents would become ever more distant in time. Neither adoption nor in vitro fertilization (IVF) requires a redefinition of parenthood, but cloning does, driving a wedge between biological and familial relationships. The clone might never have the opportunity to know their biological parents because they died long ago, leading to a crisis of identity.

It is often claimed that cloning is "just like twins." Not so. We have already noted some biological differences, but the relational differences are more profound. Twins are siblings born at the same time from the same mother. A clone would be the twin, not of a sibling, in the first instance, but of the person—the relational parent—who undertakes to care for the clone, assuming that this person is the nucleus-donor. This is twin-hood across generations, something quite different from normal twins. The relational parent will be reminded constantly as the clone grows up that the child is his or her genetic twin, but bears no genetic relationship nor resemblance to his or her partner, who may well feel excluded from the developing relationship between the nucleus-donor and the clone. Cloning represents a denial of both the asymmetry and mutuality of marriage. When the clone grows up, his or her genetically unrelated relational parent might have the unsettling experience of seeing the clone looking virtually identical to his or her partner as on the day when they first met.

The clone's sense of identity might be at risk in other ways. As Mark Phippen, head of the University of Cambridge Counselling Service, comments: "Consciously or unconsciously the nucleus-donor is bound to compare, to note the similarities and differences, to make assumptions about their child's character and abilities. . . . Psychologically, issues such as identity problems would be expected; there would likely be difficulties with the process of individuation and 'leaving home'; perhaps also with forming intimate relationships. . . ."[35] There is an issue here of human privacy and of human self-determination, which could so easily become smothered by the nucleus-donor's narcissistic tendencies.

So cloning should be opposed, not because it involves a novel reproductive technology, but because it risks establishing a new social order that fails to reflect God's image in humankind adequately. The Bible describes a God of diversity, of three-in-oneness, who has delegated stewardship responsibilities to males and females, humans in diversity, who subdue the earth, procreating and caring for their children in the context of loving married relationships. Biology and theology are in harmony, singing from the same hymn-sheet. That is God's pattern. Cloning disrupts this pattern by splitting the biology and the theology, by divorcing procreation from a loving and committed sexual union and by generating a disturbing discontinuity in sibling and parental relationships, thereby undermining family structures. Such structures are already under intense pressure, and their breakdown leads to immense personal suffering, psychologically and often physically, and to major economic costs for society.

If human clones are ever born, as they may be, then Christians should be the first to affirm their value in the sight of God. Of course a clone could become a child of God like any other person. The critique of cloning expressed here is not that a cloned person would be any different from anyone else in the sight of God, but that the proposal of cloning as an asexual human social practice threatens to undermine the relational, familial order that God has established for human well-being.

Christians should show compassion and understanding toward the plight of infertile couples, and toward those, such as the hypothetical Robinson family, who lose children under tragic circumstances. But experimenting with children, physically and psychologically, is no way to tackle infertility, and the idea that a dead child can be replaced is mistaken. Furthermore, a responsible stance toward the future structure of society has to address the question: "If many people, or even the majority, embark on this practice, then what kind of society will we be living in within the next decades?"

Ironically, it is in sex-saturated societies that the secular proposal has arisen to reproduce without sex. Biblical teaching has always emphasized the beauty and wonder of sexual union within a loving and committed relationship. The prospect of cloning now provides the Church with an opportunity to emphasize the same teaching within a totally novel context.

THERAPEUTIC CLONING

"Therapeutic cloning" is an unfortunate term that has become attached in public discourse to a procedure that has very different goals from human reproductive cloning. In the 1990s techniques were developed for growing human stem cells in the laboratory. Stem cells are the undifferentiated cells found in early embryos that have not yet started developing into the various specialized types of cell that make up the different tissues of our bodies. When a human egg is fertilized the resulting zygote undergoes three rounds of cell division until it consists of eight genetically identical cells. It is at this stage that a cell can be taken for PGD, as described earlier, because each of the cells are "totipotent" in the sense that each can develop into a complete, healthy human being. So this pre-embryo can divide into two or three portions at this stage to generate twins or triplets. By five days after conception, a hollow ball of cells, the blastocyst, has formed. The outer blastocyst cell layer goes on to form the placenta. The inner 50 or so cells are called "pluripotent stem cells" because they develop further to form the various tissues of the developing embryo. Each of these cells can give rise to most cell types, although they cannot each give rise to *all* of the 216 different cell types that make up an adult human body, which is why they are called "pluripotent" rather than "totipotent."

Recently it has been found that by growing stem cells with different growth factors they can be triggered to differentiate along certain developmental pathways to look like muscle cells or neuronal cells, for example. So the hope is that such cells could be used to repair damaged tissues in the muscles or brain or other organs of the body. In the mouse, for example, it has already been shown that embryonic stem cells can be differentiated into motor neurons, pancreatic cells or precursors of immune cells, and that these cells can be integrated into mouse tissues to restore damaged functions.[36] For example, pancreatic cells result in insulin secretion and the normalization of blood glucose levels in diabetic mice, holding out some hope that the same approach could be used in humans suffering from diabetes. Stem cell therapy has already been used to enable a blind American, Mike May, to receive back his sight, although because he lost his vision at the age of three the re-wiring of his neuronal circuits that took place in his brain since that time means that now his restoration of sight is only partial.[37] Nevertheless, this pioneering therapy holds out great hope for the future.

After development of the embryo most tissues are fully differentiated and further growth or repair of damaged sites is undertaken by the few stem cells that reside in the different tissues. Stem cells are also found in adult tissues, but in much fewer numbers—and they are also more difficult to grow in the laboratory. This contrasts with embryonic stem cells, which can be grown indefinitely. Furthermore, it is not yet clear whether adult stem cells have the same potential to develop into many different cell types: some appear to be partly differentiated already so that they do not have quite the same range of potential as stem cells obtained from embryos. Having said that, adult stem cells appear to have a broader range of options for being "re-programmed" into other cell types than originally thought.[38] In fact it has proved possible to isolate multipotent cells from the bone marrow of adult mice, rats and humans after a prolonged three-month culture period. Furthermore, it has been shown that these cells have considerable potential to develop into other cell types.[39] However, the jury is still out as to whether adult stem cells can be used therapeutically to cure a diseased tissue as has already been demonstrated for embryonic stem cells.[40]

One great advantage of using adult stem cells, apart from avoiding the ethical dilemmas that we discuss below, is that the cells could in principle be derived from the patient who is being treated. This means that there should be a perfect tissue-match for the cells grown in the laboratory that are subsequently used for therapy, so greatly decreasing the chance of tissue rejection.

It will be clear from these descriptions that growing either embryonic or adult stem cells per se does not involve "cloning." It is common practice to grow cell-lines for research, derived from various bodily tissues, often obtained originally from tumors, but the word "clone" is not generally used by scientists when referring to such cell-lines. However, there is a further step that can be carried out, and that is initially to use nuclear transfer to make a cloned embryo, genetically identical to a patient's cells. Stem cells could then be derived from this cloned embryo. The advantage of this approach is that when those embryonic stem cells are then used therapeutically to repair the patient's diseased tissue, they would not be rejected by the bodyimmune system because they would be identical to the tissues already present, so would be recognized as "self" rather than as "foreign." Those who would prefer to use only adult stem cells for therapy would respond that those cells already have this advantage built-in anyway, an argument that would become much stronger if it could be definitively demonstrated, using animal models in the first instance, that adult stem cell therapy actually works.

It will be apparent from these descriptions that the ethical issues raised by the use of therapeutic embryonic stem cells (a term that is preferable to "therapeutic cloning" for the reasons already given) are quite different from those raised by reproductive cloning. The central ethical dilemma is of course whether it is ever justifiable to use an early embryo, prior to pre-implantation, to generate embryonic stem cell-lines in the laboratory. Stem cell-lines require the death of the early embryo. Opponents of the technology draw attention to the dangers of commodification of embryos, whereby they are created only for the purpose of (eventually) healing others. This encourages a utilitarian stance toward human life, and the argument here is that "the end never justifies the means."

Some Christians also believe that each fertilized egg represents a unique human life and that God endows this life with a soul at conception. Therefore the status and value of the early embryo is equivalent to the value of the fully grown adult.[41] From the other side of the argument, those who support stem-cell therapies will point to the enormous medical potential of using the technology to relieve suffering and to heal people with diabetes, muscular dystrophy, Parkinson's disease, and so on.

The legal situation in the US relevant to stem cell therapy research and clinical application is complex. In 1995, Congress passed the Dickey Amendment, prohibiting federal funding of research that involves the use of a human embryo. However, privately funded research lead to the breakthrough that made embryonic stem cell research possible in 1998, and this prompted the Clinton Administration to develop federal regulations for its funding. President George W. Bush announced, on August 11, 2001, that for the first time federal funds would be used to support research on human embryonic stem cells, but that funding would be limited to "existing (embryonic) stem cell lines where the life-and-death decision has already been made." President Bush also stated that the federal government would continue to support research involving stem cells from other sources, such as umbilical cord blood, placentas, and adult and animal tissues. Some felt the restrictions should have been stronger, while some scientists felt frustrated with the restrictions. The Bush administration's policy does not prohibit *private* embryonic stem cell research. Pharmaceutical companies and biotechnology companies initially expressed little interest because they considered therapies based on cells, which might have to be tailored to each patient, to be less profitable than one-size-fits-all drugs. However, that situation is now changing with many start-up biotechs entering the field, such as StemCells Inc. and Aastrom Biosciences. In addition some states have decided to use state taxpayer funds for stem cell research, $3 billion in the case of California to found the California Institute for Regenerative Medicine, which opened in early 2005.

In the US, therefore, three different types of legislation impinge on stem cell therapy research: the ban on federal funding; the lack of regulation in the private sector; and the "intermediate" position of regulations arising from state-controlled funding. Unfortunately the debate in the US has become over-politicized, a trend that does not always assist informed debate. For example, it is not always realised that "spare embryos" generated at in vitro fertilization (IVF) clinics can be utilized for the generation of human stem cells.

During each round of IVF a large number of spare embryos are normally generated which are stored frozen in the event that the mother fails to become pregnant or does have a baby but then later on wishes to have another child. These spare embryos are stored for fixed periods of time and are then eventually destroyed with parental consent. However, parental consent can also be obtained for the embryos not to be destroyed but to be used to make stem cell lines. Since the spare embryos are going to be destroyed anyway, arguably it is better that they be used (potentially) to heal sick people rather than being totally wasted. Those who take this stance will point to the 80 percent "wastage" of early embryos that occurs anyway during the natural process of fertilization. Those who oppose that argument will point out that there is a big difference between what we do deliberately and what is unavoidable.[42]

As in all ethical discourse, motivation is an important factor. Some Christians would disallow the creation of an embryo with the specific aim of destroying it in order to make embryonic stem cells, but would nevertheless be open to the use of spare embryos that were created with the motivation of procreation, but were not in the end used for that purpose. While at first blush such distinctions might appear to be in the realm of how many angels can dance on a pin, Jesus' teaching in the Sermon on the Mount (for example) focuses on the motivations of our hearts and we are judged accordingly. When faced with difficult ethical dilemmas, it is the "motivation factor" that may often tip the argument one way or another.

Many Christians believe that although the early embryo deserves our care and protection to the best of our ability because it is a helpless life with all the potential to develop into an adult human given the right circumstances, nevertheless that protection may sometimes have to be balanced against equally powerful considerations of the value of other human lives. The fact that the Bible gives no clear guidance on the precise status of early embryos should make Christians cautious about being too absolutist in their claims and too harsh on those whose own convictions on the matter may not precisely match their own. Least of all should people's convictions on the matter be seen as a badge of Christian orthodoxy, as if equivalent in importance to some basic doctrine of the faith.[43]

As it happens, the ethical dilemmas raised by stem cell therapies may eventually be dissolved by further technical advances. For a start, there is already a good number of stem cell-lines in existence that can be used for research. It is possible that "tissue banks" of stem cell-lines could eventually be stored at various medical centers around the country that would be tissue-matched for virtually any patient who might come along. This would not require cloning of stem cells by nuclear transfer because the range of stem cell-lines generated could eventually cover the whole span of the major variants in tissue types that lead to transplant rejection.

It is also possible that eventually ways of using adult stem cells for therapy will come up trumps, making the use of embryonic stem cells redundant. Active research programmes on this topic are in progress in both academia and industry. As far as the biotechnology industry is concerned, a survey revealed that more than 30 biotech start-up companies in 11 different countries are pursuing commercial developments of stem cell technology.[44] These firms employ around 1,000 scientists and support staff and spend around $200 million on research and development each year. The race is on—and for readers of this book suffering from debilitating diseases, that could just prove to be some very good news. Time will tell.

A Christian reading this section on the use of therapeutic stem cells might be disappointed to find that the issues are not simply black and white. But this is not unusual in the application of modern technologies to complex issues in society. What is important is that Christians are actively involved in the ethical debate in the public arena—as they certainly are in the present debate—and that their arguments are based on accurate information. It is certainly the case that scientists might try to "steamroller" public opinion for the sake of giving complete freedom to their research activities, and by the same token companies might rush ahead for commercial gain. Christians can therefore make a vital contribution by urging time for ethical reflection and by taking a long-term view that tries to look at the "big picture," a picture that includes the key element of human relationships and the structure of the societies in which we live.

CHAPTER 8

Spaceship Earth

The advent of cheap international jet travel, and almost instantaneous communications around the world through radio, television, telephone and the internet, has meant that the perceived size of the world has shrunk steadily through the last few decades. We are now quite likely to hear through the media the result of an international cricket match on the other side of the world before we hear the outcome of a game on our own village green, just down the road.

In tandem with this growth in speed of communication has been the rapid development of activities that have truly global effects. This is particularly the case for those emanating from the high-income countries. In the political sphere, superpowers such as the US are able to force their will on smaller nations on the other side of the world, either through financial pressure or by overwhelming force of arms. In the economic realm, globalization means that a few huge companies, some with incomes higher than entire nation states, are able to exercise transnational cultural and economic influence with little real control by individual national governments. And in the environmental arena, it is clear that the effects of pollutants pumped into the atmosphere by a small sector of the world's population as a by-product of a consumer society may cause unprecedented rates of global climate change; and that ecological changes, caused, for example, by deforestation and land-use changes, are leading to the extinction of species at a rate ten to a hundred times above the normal level, a rate only rarely before experienced on earth through hundreds of millennia.

We truly live on a spaceship earth. What people do in one part of the world affects others, everywhere. It is no longer possible to assume, for example, that the oceans are so large that they can soak up all our waste without any deleterious effects. Nor can we escape the fact that lifestyle choices in the high-income parts of the world impact directly on the economic and living conditions experienced by hundreds of millions of people elsewhere in the world. We live in a world of finite size and resources and one which for the first time in history may be approaching its maximum population carrying capacity.

What should be the Christian response to these issues of global change? First, it should be said that it is pointless to try to turn the clock back to an earlier, agrarian age. Even if that could be done (which it could not, other than as a consequence of some catastrophic war or environmental disaster that destroyed society and government as we know it), we would find that life in the pre-industrial era was considerably worse than it is now. Few will deny the benefits of the alleviation of human suffering that has been brought about by advances in medicine, by improved food production and distribution, by better education and communications. Yet there remains the apparent contradiction that it is the very development of technology allowed by improved scientific understanding of the material world that has brought with it those undesirable hangers-on of pollution, of environmental degradation, and all the unpleasant side effects experienced by the majority of the world's population who live in the low-income regions.

Before we address specifically Christian responses to these various global issues, we need to say that Christians cannot simply walk away from their responsibility to address them head-on. The Bible is clear on the imperative for Christians to concern themselves with the physical as well as the spiritual well-being of others, and particularly of those least able to speak out or to act for themselves. It is also clear, as we have pointed out in earlier chapters, that God's call to humankind is for us to be good stewards of God's creation, both to use the resources of the world for the common good and to act, as it were, as on God's behalf. So we need to examine the theological basis for the Christian attitude before we discuss appropriate Christian responses to particular global issues.

A "new heaven" and a "new earth"

From beginning to end the Bible underlines the innate goodness of God's creation. As already highlighted, the very first chapters of Genesis at the beginning of the Bible underscore the fact that God created a material world that was good: after every act of creation, God proclaimed pleasure with every aspect of it, from the mightiest stars to the most humble starfish. It is also clear that all of creation is under God's sovereignty: God willed it into existence from nothing, ex nihilo,[1] and upholds it moment by moment. When God came to creating man and woman, God was especially pleased: God pronounced them to be "*very good*" and gave them considerable authority over, and care for, the created world. This points to the very special place of humankind in God's created order.

There is no sense here that God is in any way limited by the constraints of the material creation. God would continue to exist even if the created universe did not. Nor is there any sense that God's material creation is less than the best God willed for it. It is a mistake to fall into the trap of thinking that material things are any less important to God, or any less near to God, than so-called "spiritual" matters. There is no encouragement at all in the Bible to believe that we should strive to put the material world behind us, or to subjugate it in favour of some supposedly greater or higher spiritual plane.

If the Genesis account of creation insists that at the beginning God's created material world was good, then the later biblical narratives draw attention to, first, the way in which that creation has been marred by humankind's selfishness and rebellion against God the creator and, second, a future restoration of the universe when it will be perfected to how God always intended it to be. Assuredly, our present world is not perfect. We are surrounded daily by images of death and destruction, by reports of inhuman behavior by humans, by the universal experience of suffering and pain—not experienced all the time by all people, but clearly at least some of the time, by every individual.

The Bible offers a clear assessment of this paradox. We live in what is at root a wonderfully coherent and fertile universe, with humankind capable of expressing the heights of beauty and love. Yet it is also at times a messy, painful place. The reason for this, the authors of the Bible say with a consistent voice, is that this malfunctioning of individuals and of human society, and even of the created world, is the consequence of humankind's selfish nature: in theological terms it is due to humankind turning away from the proper relationship of trust and obedience that created beings ought to have with God their creator, and instead assuming a mantle of self-determination, of rejection of their creator. The Christian gospel is that Jesus has made possible a restoration of that perfect relationship with God, provided only that individuals turn back from their former rejection of God and instead accept God's rightful place as creator and ruler of the universe. And one day in the future, God will bring an end to this present world and will usher in a new universe with the fullness of life always intended and purposed for creation: a place where people will truly be at home.

The flow of scripture, from an original perfect created order to a recreated perfect order in the world to come, is crucial to understanding and to determining our response in the world in which we live now, between the beginning and the end of this narrative.[2] The Bible itself captures this flow: the very first chapter of Genesis at the beginning of the Bible describes the goodness and purposefulness of God's creative activity; the very last two chapters in Revelation at the end of the Bible provide a wonderful picture of "a new heaven and a new earth,"[3] where God dwells with humanity, and where there is "no more death or mourning or crying or pain, for the old order of things has passed away."[4] Yet the great bulk of the Bible sandwiched between these end pieces concerns itself with how we should live now, in the light of the created origin and the future goal of the universe.

The Bible writers continually look forward to this renewed world, and throughout both the Old Testament (e.g., Isaiah)[5]and the New Testament (e.g., Paul's letters to the Romans; the letter to the Hebrews; Peter's second letter),[6] remind us of the future "new heaven and new earth." But they are also clear that in the present, flawed world the Christian needs to work at using the material world for good. The certain hope of a renewed future creation is not a license to abandon care for this one. Rather, the opposite is the case: because there is a continuity between this world and the next, because it will be the fulfillment of God the creator's good plans for this universe, then there is every incentive to foster and to use the innate underlying goodness and fruitfulness of this material world to do what is pleasing to God in our time and place.

There is a strong sense of continuity in scripture between this current world and the future one. It is as if the new creation in the future will be the full reality and that we live in a faint shadow of it now. Tom Wright, in his commentary on the biblical picture of the Christian hope in the new heaven and new earth,[7] likens it to a child's Christmas presents kept in a cupboard in the days leading up to Christmas: there is no doubt that they are there, and that they are solid and real, but they are being kept safe in that cupboard awaiting the day to which the child is looking forward when he will receive them. In a similar vein, we can think of God keeping the full reality of the future perfected life "safe" in heaven until the time is right for us to experience it in its fullness.[8] It is no less real for the fact that we cannot see it today, although we can perhaps catch glimpses of it from time to time.

The physical continuity between this world and the next is emphasized by the biblical descriptions of heaven. Although the Bible writers may be struggling to describe a place that is beyond full description in our earth-bound, limited terms, yet still they paint a picture of a place where we will feel completely at home, where we will have recognizable physical bodies, where we will know one another, and where we will love and be loved. The surroundings will be ones of intense physical beauty and well-being: the lion will lie down with the lamb, there will be the fragrance of flowers, the shade of trees, the sense of all being right with the world. All these, and more, are things that we may experience in our present life in a transient sense: in heaven this will be the steady, settled reality always.

There is no sense here of the populist view of heaven as a place where disembodied spirits float around in a nebulous, spiritual realm. Nor is this a pie-in-the-sky utopia. The decisions we make in this world, the things we do and say, our personalities, will all in some sense carry forward to the world to come. There is no doubt that they will be purified (as if "with fire" says Paul in his letter to the Corinthians[9]) and transformed, with the hardness, selfishness, acquisitiveness and flaws stripped away: but still the Bible is crystal clear that how we behave in this world has a bearing on the next. It would not be surprising if our restoration to being the kind of earth-keepers that God expects us to be in the present world were to be matched by equally weighty responsibilities in the new creation.[10]

In this context it is intriguing that the new heaven and earth are represented in the New Testament not only by a restored garden—which is what you might expect from the first few chapters of Genesis—but also by a city. The city is the place of human community, creativity and technology and the "glory and honor of the nations will be brought into it."[11] Given God's passion for creating wonderful objects out of materials, an ability that has been in part imparted to us, it is difficult to believe that the most beautiful and God-honoring technical creations will not comprise at least part of that great wealth that finds its continuity in the new earth.

We catch a further glimpse of the future physical reality in the reports of the appearances of Jesus to his disciples and to many hundreds of other people shortly after his resurrection. He is the only person who has ever come back from heaven to earth, so was perhaps purposely showing us something of that reality. When he appeared to these people he had a new, physical body. He ate food like other people, and people could speak with him, could touch him and could feel him. Indeed, so normal was his appearance that one pair of rather dejected disciples walking home from Jerusalem shortly after the first Easter day thought that Jesus was just another stranger on the road and fell into a long conversation with him about the events of the previous days.[12] Jesus' resurrection body also had other unusual properties. Apparently he could appear and disappear within locked rooms, as he did when he met the disciples shortly after his resurrection.[13] Not only could he appear and disappear at will, but when he finally left the earth six weeks after he had risen, he did so without leaving behind a physical body. So although in form and physical appearance he was fully a man, God is showing us that God can use the physical material of this created world in whatever way God chooses: if we have a robust view of God as creator and sustainer of the universe then there is nothing surprising in this. We tend to call such things "supernatural," but in truth they are just part of God's nature and God is showing us power over the stuff of the created universe.

To come back to ground, as it were, we return to consider how this understanding of God's stated purposes for the new heaven and new earth should affect our present behavior in this world. First, this under- lying knowledge that God's created universe is good, that the material world that scientists investigate as their bread-and-butter activity is ba- sically good, should drive scientists to keep striving to understand the stuff of this world as well as they can. We may not discover "the mind of god" by doing science, as Stephen Hawking memorably suggested of the search for a Grand Unified Theory in physics,[14] but we certainly will learn how to use this material world better in serving others and by extension, therefore, in serving God.

Second, we need to keep in mind that this created world is marred by humankind's disobedience to God the creator. We therefore need to be wary because people are quite capable of using the power inherent in our understanding of this world for great evil as well as for great good. We should not live in cloud-cuckoo-land about the dangers of scientific knowledge and need to act as responsible stewards of that knowledge, helping to put in place constraints on its use where appropriate.

Third, it is obvious that we should not worship the physical world or anything in it, because it represents only the created things and not the creator. Nor should we strive unduly to acquire the possessions of this world, partly because they are only transient and will one day pass away, but equally clearly they will not be of any use to us in the future ei- ther. Such may be obvious, but that doesn't seem to prevent many people, and even whole nations, spending their lives in the pursuit of something that is ultimately not only unattainable (because it is owned by God), but is strictly transient both on a human time frame and from God's perspective of the new heaven and new earth.

Fourth, and perhaps most positively, an understanding of the con- tinuity of the future heaven and earth with this world should lead us to live and to work in this world—as far as it is possible—in a way that mir- rors or prefigures the way we shall live in the world to come. If this world is a paler version of a fuller, more real world to come, then the way we behave in this world and the way we treat this world should prefigure the way it will be when God has cleansed and restored both creation and humanity. Our concern for the environment now on planet earth in relation to the environment of the new heaven and the new earth is like that between a pilot plant and its fulfillment in the final operation that it is intended to model. What we do now is not merely limited to a world that is going to be destroyed, but has eternal significance in being inextricably linked to the new world which God one day is going to bring into being.

The key question, then, for us is: "Are we, right now, in the present, being good stewards of all that God has delegated to us?" This is a charter that sees equal dangers in freezing the resources of the world and saying that we should not disturb them, as in despoiling the natural environment for short-term gain. We need to find a middle ground for stewarding the earth, looking to the needs of both our present generation and of those to come. A good illustration of this is given by Martin Luther's remark that, "If I knew Jesus would return tomorrow, I would plant a tree today." This is a powerful picture of how we should behave as Christians in this world: a good touchstone of our daily activities is whether, if we knew we were to die tomorrow, we would still do the same things today. All that we do as Christians here on planet earth has potential to be part of our worship. As we obey God and care for the world committed to our care, so we worship God. Obedience is part of worship. And the present world and our delegated roles within it are of value in and of themselves.

With that in mind we look next at four topical issues of rapid global change and of appropriate Christian responses to them: the natural environment, global climate change, sustainable development and globalization.

The natural environment

Although this may come as a surprise to those who think that a Christian view of how we deal with God's world is disdainful of this world, which will "pass away," Christians have a firmer theological basis and a more powerful motivation for caring for the environment than is provided by any other world religion or New Age philosophy. The picture that the first few chapters of Genesis paint for us is of humans placed in a beautiful garden with the task of caring for it, obtaining food from it, and organizing its flora and fauna.[15] The word generally used for "man" in the Old Testament is *ish*, but the writer of Genesis deliberately chose an alternative word for "man"—*Adam*—to make a Hebrew pun on man who was made from the *adama*—the "ground" (Genesis 2:7). Adam and Eve are portrayed as God's earth-keepers. When they sinned against God, one consequence was that they no longer lived in harmony with the *adama* over which God had put them in charge.[16]

The Protestant reformer John Calvin in 1554 C.E. described vividly the Christian basis for our care for the environment in his commentary on Genesis chapter 2, verse 15:

> The earth was given to man, with this condition, that he should occupy himself in its cultivation. . . . The custody of the garden was given in charge to Adam, to show that we possess the things which God has committed to our hands, on the condition that, being content with the frugal and moderate use of them, we should take care of what shall remain. Let him who possesses a field, so partake of its yearly fruits, that he may not suffer the ground to be injured by his negligence, but let him endeavour to hand it down to posterity as he received it, or even better cultivated. Let him so feed on its fruits, that he neither dissipates it by luxury, nor permits it to be marred or ruined by neglect. Moreover, that this economy, and this diligence, with respect to those good things which God has given us to enjoy, may flourish among us, let everyone regard himself as the steward of God in all things which he possesses. Then he will neither conduct himself dissolutely, nor corrupt by abuse those things which God requires to be preserved.[17]

If only the powerful teaching expressed in these words had been applied consistently over the intervening centuries, then the world in which we live now would be a very different place. To be fair to our predecessors, however, it is worth emphasizing that in many cases they simply did not realize the damage that they were doing to the environment. The huge oceans and untamed wilderness with its vast forests and impenetrable swamps were so huge in comparison with a relatively small human population that any effects of human actions appeared trivial by comparison. In pre-agricultural times the total world population was probably fewer than 10 million and even by Roman times had increased to only 300 million. The intimate connections between food chains, the effects on climate of burning fossil fuels, the link between the destruction of forests and drought, were not understood well until the twentieth century. Ironically, one of the greatest naturalists of all time, Charles Darwin, regularly shot and ate the species that he was so busy describing. But as Darwin visited the great jungles of South America during his nineteenth-century voyage on the Beagle, he could never have imagined the devastation of that environment a mere 150 years later.

At the beginning of the twenty-first century, things look very different. Humans are now by far the biggest cause of change on the earth. They are responsible for moving more earth materials per year (for housing, roads, mining and the like), than all the natural processes of the world added together. The average amount of earth material moved per year is estimated as about 30 tons per person in the US, and 6 tons per person averaged across the whole world. This produces a total of about 35,000 million tons per year moved by humans worldwide at the present, compared to 15,000–20,000 million tons of sediment carried to the oceans by all the rivers of the world combined. The volume of earth material moved by humankind over the past 5,000 years would be sufficient to build an artificial mountain 4,000 meters high, 40 kilometers wide and 100 kilometers long and, at the present rate of increase, it would double in length over the next 100 years.[18] In addition, deforestation and agriculture have increased the flow of soil and sediments along rivers into the oceans by a factor of 2 to 10 times since humans began farming.[19] Biologically, humankind is responsible for massive extinction of species, exceeding the normal rate of species turnover in the geological record of the earth by a factor of 10 to 100. Climatically, the current projected rate of change of global temperature caused by humans is without precedent in the history of the last 10,000 years of the world. And the population of the world continues to grow exceedingly rapidly: in just one lifetime of three score years and ten it has tripled. Humankind is having an unprecedented impact on the environment.

Global climate change

This issue is particularly relevant in contemporary debate about care for the environment. It is a topic of broad societal and international importance and is being addressed vigorously by secular groups and (perhaps less vigorously) by governments. It is also an issue where Christians have strong contributions to make from their foundational beliefs in the creator God.

It has become apparent over the past decade that the average temperature of the surface of the earth is rising slowly, but inexorably, as a direct result of human activities. Mostly this is due to the burning of fossil fuels such as oil, gas and coal in industrialized societies, although the rapid increase in the earth's population is also a contributory factor. A highly respected independent panel of over 600 scientific experts from all over the world under the auspices of the United Nations and the

Variations of the earth's surface temperature for the past 1,000 years

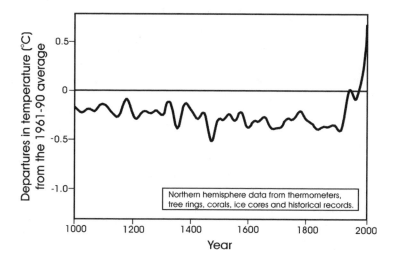

World Meteorological Office has examined a large variety of different likely scenarios for the temperature changes to be expected over the coming years: the best predictions are that the average global surface temperature will rise by 1.4–5.8°C over the period 1990–2100, and that sea level will rise by 9–88 centimeters over the same period,[20] although recent models show that both the temperature increase and the sea-level rise in some scenarios may be considerably greater.

An average temperature rise of just a few degrees, and a sea-level rise of less than a meter, even in the worst case, does not at first sight seem very significant or bad. However, accompanying the climate changes are rapid changes in climate patterns, and particularly in extreme weather events such as cyclones, and in variability of the monsoons that so much of the low-income world depends on for agriculture. And the risk of drought is likely to become much greater over most mid-latitude continental interiors. The problem is not so much in the change of these climate patterns as in the extreme rapidity of those changes, which is far greater than the world has experienced over the past 10,000 years, and to which it is extremely hard for settled human populations to respond. The consequence is likely to be a huge increase in the numbers of environmental refugees, people displaced from their homelands by drought or flood or starvation.

Take, for example, the nation of Bangladesh, one of the poorest in the world, but with a population of more than 120 million. One quarter of the habitable land is less than 3 meters (10 feet) above sea level, and 30 million people live in that area. By 2050, a 1 meter rise in relative sea level is predicted, with about one-third of that being due to global warming, and two-thirds to land subsidence caused primarily by the removal of ground-water for drinking and irrigation. By 2100, the relative rise in sea level is predicted to have doubled to 2 meters. As anyone who has stood on the sea shore watching the waves will know, the problem is not just the average rise in sea level encroaching on the land, but the occasional storms which cause sea water to surge inland: they cause not only a temporary flooding, often with loss of life by drowning, but the salt water also ruins the land for agriculture. In November 1970, one of the biggest natural disasters known in the world occurred in Bangladesh, when more than a quarter of a million people died by drowning in a storm surge.[21] Though high-income nations with the resources to cope can respond to sea-level rises by building flood barriers, such as the Thames Barrier in England, or the dykes and sea defenses of The Netherlands,[22] this is simply not an option for a low-income country such as Bangladesh with its convoluted, deltaic coastline. And since worldwide

Predicted variations of the earth's surface temperature: last 1,000 and next 100 years

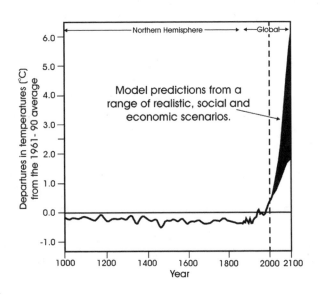

about one-half of humanity lives in coastal zones, sea-level rise is a huge problem globally. As well as in Bangladesh, huge numbers of people will be displaced in southern China, and many islands in the Indian and Pacific oceans are likely to become uninhabitable as a result of sea-level rise.

The issue of environmental refugees is one that has rarely been considered in the past: indeed many governments, although ready to consider admitting refugees who are at risk of physical torture or oppression if they returned to their homelands, are unwilling to admit so-called "economic" refugees. Yet even today, there are estimated to be more environmental refugees (at least 25 million), than refugees of the traditional kind (about 22 million). And the number of environmental refugees is likely to double by or before 2010. It is, of course, the poorest who are most at risk. Almost one-quarter of the world's population survives on less than $1 per day, and right now over 140 million people are threatened by severe desertification, and another 550 million are subject to chronic water shortages.[23] Rapid climate change only exacerbates the environmental problems, including drought, soil erosion, desertification and deforestation faced by many hundreds of millions of people.

No country can cope easily with huge numbers of environmental refugees arriving in a very short period because they bring alien cultures, customs and living habits that are difficult to integrate into the existing society. And as with all refugees, the tragedy of enforced migration is made worse by the break-up of traditional family and community relationships and patterns of social cohesion rooted to the areas in which people have grown up and lived. So there is an urgent need to stabilize climate changes so as to minimize such rapid and deleterious changes to the environment. It will not make the problems of the poor and the under-resourced go away, but it will at least remove one terrifying aspect of their lives, that of enforced uprooting from their marginalized homelands due to climate change.

Before we leave the issue of environmental refugees, it is worth remembering that the Bible has a lot to say about caring for the stranger in our midst. Although our natural reaction tends to be to shun the outsider, while heaving a sigh of relief that it isn't oneself in that predicament, the Old Testament has much useful and pithy instruction on how to treat strangers, who in the context were usually the refugees of their time.[24] Foremost among them is to treat strangers as yourselves (Leviticus 19:34), and to love the foreigner in your midst (Deuteronomy 10:19), a command which is reinforced by Jesus" injunction to "Love your neighbour as yourself" (Mark 12:31). In practical terms, this means providing them with sufficient help to enable them to continue to live among you (Leviticus 25:35), ensuring that you do not discriminate against them, so that they are subject to the same laws as yourselves (Leviticus 24:22), and being generous in welfare provision (Leviticus 19:9; 23:22).

Returning now to the issue of climate change, it is clear that the high-income nations have had a disproportionate share of the benefits derived from the industrialization which itself is primarily responsible for global warming, while the most deleterious effects are likely to be suffered by the lowest-income nations, which are least able to cope with rapid changes. For example, 25 percent of the entire world production of the main greenhouse gas (carbon dioxide) that is responsible for global warming is produced by the US alone. Therefore common justice demands that those responsible should take the lead at least in preventing further worsening of the damage. This is not a trivial undertaking: even if the entire greenhouse gas production were stabilized today, changes in climate would persist for many centuries. This is because the gases persist for very long periods in the atmosphere and the huge mass of the oceans takes so long to absorb heat—and so the sea level will continue to rise over hundreds of years into the future.[25]

The world community has recognized the global nature of this problem for more than a decade. After years of planning and negotiation, this had led to a notable achievement when delegates from 160 countries meeting in 1992 in Rio de Janeiro under the auspices of the United Nations agreed to take action to return the emissions of greenhouse gases, and particularly of carbon dioxide, to their 1990 levels. It was understood at that meeting that the main burden of this would fall on the high-income countries. Over a series of subsequent meetings of parties to the Climate Convention, culminating in one in Kyoto, Japan, in 1997, agreement was reached to aim to reduce emission by 2012 of the main greenhouse gases by an average of 5.2 percent of their 1990 levels. Detailed discussions then ensued about how exactly to implement this objective, nation by nation. Though the Kyoto agreement was signed in 1997 by Bill Clinton, then president of the US, in 2001 the new president, George W. Bush withdrew the US from the agreement, saying that he would not agree to a measure that would "harm the economy and hurt American workers." Following that withdrawal, the remaining nations of the world continued negotiations on the Kyoto Protocol, reaching agreement which opened the way to ratification in more than 180 countries. With the exception of the US, the world has agreed to the most complex environmental treaty yet, and the first that is legally binding.

How should Christians react to such developments? Once a global problem such as climate change has been identified, Christians should then be alert to the circumstances of those least able to care for themselves, even if they happen to be on the other side of the world, and of the responsibilities for taking measures to alleviate their suffering, even if it is at a material cost to ourselves or to our societies. Christians should also take the lead to lobby for appropriate responses. As Jesus taught, from those to whom a lot has been given, much will be required.[26] One day we will be called to account for our actions, or lack of them.

The consequences of climate change are long term, even if extremely immediate to those suffering the effects of a tornado or storms caused by El Niño. Politicians, at least in democracies, tend to have short-term goals and memories, but to be responsive to public opinion—not least because they are dependent on the populace for re-election. One thing Christians can therefore do is to keep the long-term issues of climate change, the impacts on other people, and the responsibilities of the industrialized nations, prominently at the forefront of public awareness. To do this they need to be well informed, and there is obviously a mandate for scientists, who should be in the best position to understand the technical issues, to take a lead in this.

Another proper response is to seek common ways forward that will benefit all those involved. Christians are called to be peacemakers and reconcilers, and it is appropriate that they should use their knowledge and skills to work for changes that will truly be of the widest benefit. But this will not just happen automatically or easily against the vested interests of the powerful, be they individuals, corporations or nations. As an example, the life's work of Wilberforce in the abolition of the slave trade, resulted in his being reviled and even hated by some because much of their wealth was built on slavery. In the same way, taking measures to reduce harmful emissions of greenhouse gases will cost money and resources in the short term: and the natural response of fallen humankind is to look first to self-interest. Christians need to be active in the world in pressing the case for the powerless and the voiceless.

When Jesus sent out his disciples he told them to be "as shrewd as snakes and as innocent as doves."[27] Likewise, we should be alert to ways within our society and culture that we can use to foster the paths of justice and of peace. Wilberforce suffered numerous setbacks in the Houses of Parliament (in 1789, 1791, 1792, 1793, 1797, 1799, 1804 and 1805) before a bill was passed to grant freedom to slaves. It was only in February 1807, when it was pointed out that the slave trade assisted Great Britain's enemies, that a bill abolishing the slave trade was passed by an overwhelming 283 votes to 16.[28] In a similar vein, in the context of climate change we can point to enlightened self-interest in taking action now to reduce emissions. The argument is that spending money now will save greater costs later: this is an argument that can be used irrespective of religious commitments or lack of them, since it appeals directly to common self-interest.

Although estimates are hard to make, and of course carry considerable uncertainty, most studies suggest that a doubling of atmospheric carbon dioxide concentrations from their pre-industrial levels will cause a loss of 1–1.5 percent of Gross National Product (GNP) for a high-income country and about 5 percent, or possibly as much as 10 percent, for a low-income country. (Low-income countries are much worse affected because their bigger dependence on agriculture and water resources makes them more vulnerable to climate change.) The average across the whole world suggests a future loss of 1.5–2 percent of the Gross World Product due to a doubling of carbon dioxide. Things get much worse if carbon dioxide increases are higher: if concentrations were to increase twice as much as assumed above, the financial cost is estimated as being 3–4 times as much, at 4–6 percent of the Gross World Product.[29] And these, of course, are only the strictly financial costs of climate change. The cost in terms of loss of species, of lost natural amenities, and of human misery and suffering is impossible to quantify in financial terms.

Is a doubling of atmospheric carbon dioxide likely? It certainly is, if we take no action to prevent it. Already, humankind has caused global atmospheric carbon dioxide to increase, by almost one-third from pre-industrial concentrations, to a level that has not been exceeded during the past half a million years, and probably not for the past 20 million years. And if we maintain a "business as usual" mentality, a doubling of carbon dioxide levels will have been reached by the middle of this century—within the life-span of the majority of people alive today.

What about the cost of stabilizing carbon dioxide emissions? If action is taken over the next 20–30 years or so to take advantage of the normal replacement of infrastructure, the likely cost is less than 1 percent of the GNP, and may be little more than half of that. This is much less than the predicted economic cost of allowing greenhouse gas production to continue unchecked, even considering only the strictly financial costs, without the burden of human misery that would result.

So there are strong financial arguments, easily understood even in a secular context, for taking action now to address climate change. There are of course other Christian and ethical incentives to do so, on some of which we have already touched. One clear imperative is that of international and intergenerational equity. The Bible often alludes to the responsibilities of parents to their children, of one generation to its successors. An approach that embodies these responsibilities has come to be called "Sustainable Development," and it is to this idea that we turn next.

Carbon dioxide for the last 160,000 years and the next 100 years

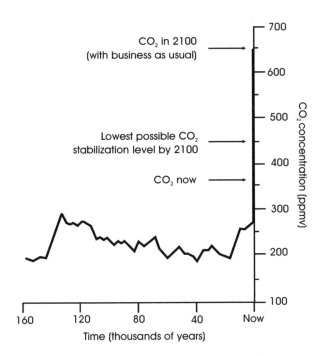

CO₂ in 2100
(with business as usual)

Lowest possible CO₂
stabilization level by 2100

CO₂ now

CO₂ concentration (ppmv)

Time (thousands of years)

Sustainable development

The concept of stewardship is ingrained in the creation order from the earliest times: in Genesis humans were placed in a garden, the Garden of Eden, "to work it and to take care of it" (Genesis 2:15).[30] Sustainable consumption, the idea that we are accountable to future generations to leave the world in more than just a barely habitable state, is a popular viewpoint at the beginning of the twenty-first century. However, the concept was already described by John Calvin rather precisely back in the sixteenth century in the passage already cited earlier. Today it is clear that science is a crucial ally in developing strategies and technologies for sustainable development.

Sustainable development has been defined by the World Commission on Environment and Development as "development that meets the needs of the present without compromising the ability of future generations to meet their own needs." In his Reith lecture of 2000, Christopher Patten described it rather more pithily as "living here as though we were intending to stay for good, not just for the weekend," a similar sentiment to that expressed by Sir Crispen Tickell who has said that we should "treat the earth as if we mean to stay." Margaret Thatcher's version was that "we do not hold a freehold on our world, but only a full repairing lease. We have a moral duty to look after our world and to hand it on in good order to future generations."

Issues raised by sustainable development apply to the problems of global climate change discussed in the previous section, but equally to the broader fields of security of access to food, forestry, water, energy, work, housing and other basic human needs. It is a concept that was second nature to our forebears a millennium ago. Settled agricultural communities knew full well the need not to despoil the land on which they depended for crops. Thus medieval strip-farming used a pattern of crop rotation and fallow periods to ensure that the land remained fertile. But on the other hand, the rapid industrialization of the world since Victorian times has made it possible to use up global resources at a rate unprecedented in the history of the world. For example, the efficiency of modern fish-finding techniques using echo-sounders and satellite imagery, together with industrialized methods of fishing, means that it is almost trivially easy to completely destroy the fish stock of a region. It is for this reason that fishing quota systems are in such widespread use. Before the international moratorium on commercial whaling, the world came within a whisker of hunting whales to extinction, in the same manner as it has already destroyed many other species.

Although few Christians would disagree with the creation mandate to be stewards of the world's resources, it is worth reminding ourselves again that this is not an easy or necessarily straightforward option. We live in a fallen world, and there are immediate consequences of that which affect the task of stewardship. We do well to bear these in mind as we grapple to promote Christian ways forward in our society.

A major consequence of the Fall is that relationships both between people, and between humans and God, have been tainted and damaged by the prevalent tendency to sinfulness, to self-interest. The practical outworking of this is that cooperating together for the common good of others is made more difficult. Yet of course most stewardship issues involve corporate responsibilities, and the realization that what we do affects other people. The difficulty of getting even a small measure of international agreement on the global climate change protocols points up the magnitude of the task of overcoming self-interest for the long-term common good. Added to the innate tendency of humans to put self-interest first is the difficulty of communicating across cultural and language barriers,[31] which easily translates into suspicion of others' motives. So Christians need not only to support the concepts of sustainable development, as indeed also do many non-Christians, but to be aware of the inherent pitfalls of human nature and to ensure that adequate safeguards are in place to counter the worst excesses.

At the start of the third millennium, the Old Testament laws on property and on land are particularly relevant in the lessons they may teach us for concepts of sustainable development. In the settled society of Israel, the land on which one lived was the source of one's livelihood, and particularly of one's food. So there were specific regulations that every 50 years (the year of Jubilee), the land should be restored to the family that originally owned it. Land could not be sold permanently under this regulation, only leased for the balance of the period to the next year of Jubilee, at a price dependent on the number of crop-producing years remaining until then. One of the graphic theological lessons from this, as God explained through Moses, was that "The land must not be sold permanently, because the land is mine and you are but aliens and my tenants" (Leviticus 25:23).[32] This specific regulation may not be directly applicable in our very different society today, and, indeed, even at the time the regulations were given, a distinction was drawn between land and property in the country—which was essential for growing foodstuffs and which were therefore subject to the Jubilee regulations—and town properties—which it was permissible to sell permanently to someone else. However, the ideas underpinning the Jubilee regulation, of the right of successive generations to have the natural resources available to sustain their normal living standards, and of God's perspective that we are temporary tenants of this world rather than in any sense owning it individually for ourselves, are particularly helpful in considering a Christian response to sustainable development. If we take good care of the world and its natural resources, and hand it on to our successors in a good state for them to use, we should do so because it is God's world, and that is what he asks of us as his stewards here.

The biblical perspective continually reinforces the view that the material riches that we enjoy are for our use during our lifetimes, and that they are loaned to us, as it were, on trust from God. The Bible is full of warnings that loving these material things too much for their own sakes can be a snare and a trap. When a rich young man, a religious and upright citizen, asked Jesus what he should do to enter heaven, Jesus told him to go and sell his possessions and give the money to the poor—the rich man went away sad. It is this very seductiveness of material goods that led Jesus to explain to his disciples just after the exchange with the rich young man that "it is easier for a camel to go through the eye of a needle than for a rich man to enter the kingdom of God."[33] This should not really come as a surprise: it is self-evident that everyone will die one day, and that all the material goods that we may have at that time will make no difference to that stark fact.

As a result of humankind's disobedience, God pronounced that humans would have to toil to bring the land to bear fruit, in contrast to its former fruitfulness.[34] So, as another consequence of the Fall, it does not necessarily come easy to use nature, even for good ends. Maybe this is why making use of science is often a costly exercise, in time, expenditure of resources, and sometimes even in human life.

The provisions of an adequate, secure food supply for all the world's population brings many of these issues into sharp focus. On a global scale, there is sufficient food for everyone. Indeed, between the mid-1960s and the end of the 1990s the calorific value of food production worldwide increased faster than the population. The average amount of food available per person worldwide increased nearly 20 percent over this period, largely due to improved crops, better agricultural practices and more effective pest control. Because the countries that had not been industrialized started from a lower base, the increase in those countries over this period exceeded 30 percent, whereas in the industrialized countries it was less than 15 percent. Nevertheless, the average food consumption in the industrialized countries in the year 2000 (3,400 kilocalories per capita), exceeded that in the developing countries by 25 percent, and is a massive 54 percent higher than in the poorest regions of the world like sub-Saharan Africa.[35] There remains the problem of the equitable distribution of resources, about which the Christian ethic has a lot to say.

The other side of the coin of development is consumption. And human behavior is such that over-consumption is endemic, even when it becomes deleterious to the health of the individual. It is a well-known observation that riches don't necessarily bring happiness: neither does an abundance of food necessarily bring healthiness. The endemic proportion of obesity in the US and, increasingly, in Western Europe, point to the power of desire even over self-interest.

In the light of human behavior, how can sustainable consumption be encouraged? It is a complex topic so there are no quick fixes. But the elements of a sustainable way forward must include: policy decisions at governmental level on taxation and subsidies; technological improvements in agriculture, storage and movement of foodstuffs; a proper costing of the full economic costs of the human and natural capital used in production and of the environmental costs of the activities; and, perhaps most important of all, a change in the behavior of individuals through education and a societal desire for change.

It is the last of these issues, the need for a change in the behavior of people, that holds out the highest hope of real change. Ultimately, democratic societies respond to the common will of the people, though often slowly and with many false turns. And people can and do change. A good example is the widespread revulsion at the massacre, on 13 March 1996, at a Dunblane primary school in Scotland of 16 young children and their teacher by an unbalanced individual with semi-automatic guns. By the next year legislation had been passed in the United Kingdom banning the private ownership of handguns above .22 caliber and the restriction of smaller caliber guns to secure gun clubs. The ban extended to guns owned for peaceful purposes such as competition target shooting. Such was the strength of feeling over the massacre that people were willing to forgo the right to a legitimate ownership of guns because of the inherent danger that a tiny minority of individuals might misuse them. It resulted ultimately in more than 200,000 guns being taken out of circulation in Great Britain.

Another example from the United States is the increasingly widespread ban in public spaces of smoking, which has come about over the past two decades. By 2005 seven states and nearly two hundred local governments nationwide supported a total ban on smoking in restaurants and bars. This is a slow, and ongoing process, brought about by long-term education about the health risks of smoking, coupled with legislative changes which increased taxation of tobacco, forced tobacco companies to print explicit health warnings on cigarette packs and finally banned tobacco advertising. So people can and do change their behavior, for complex reasons which include both their own self-interest, social pressures and the wider interests of others.

The way to develop sustainable consumption and sustainable development practices is likely to be similar to the path followed in removing cigarette smoking from public places: a combination of education, of changed individual practices and of legislative direction through taxes, subsidies and advertising. For the Christian, although the main reason for desiring changes to a sustainable lifestyle individually and corporately may come from their theological understanding of the relationship between God, creation and themselves, such changes are most likely to be achieved in a secular environment by showing the ultimate benefits to the long-term economic, security and health prospects for society. If the changes are truly in line with God's creation mandate, as we believe sustainable development and consumption practices to be, then they will inevitably lead to benefits overall: living in the way God intended in the creation that God made is bound to be better than working at odds with it. Square pegs in round holes never fit well.

Globalization

Globalization is an issue widely bandied around by the chattering classes, by politicians and by activists, but it is one of those ill-defined terms that can mean, as Humpty Dumpty said, "just what I choose it to mean." Often enough it is used as a shorthand for "Americanization," and then usually in a derogatory sense. Yet at root it is clear that it encompasses a growing awareness that almost instantaneous global communications and easy international travel have allowed relatively small groups of people or corporations the power to dominate large sectors of the world in economic, political and cultural spheres. That in itself is not necessarily a bad thing, although human nature being what it is, the outcome is often that the rich get richer and the poor, poorer.

From a Christian perspective, the issues that need to be addressed in considering the effects of globalization are primarily ones of justice (whether the rich parties use their technological advantage to downtread the poorer parties), and of equity (whether material resources are being fairly shared). The dominant driving force of globalization is the profit motive: corporations exist primarily to deliver profits to their shareholders, so it is in their interests to drive down the costs of raw materials such as timber, minerals, oil, coffee and bananas. God's economy is based on different values: Jesus reminds us (in John 10:10) that we should delight in the goodness and richness of God's creation, while ensuring for the care of the poor, the widow and the orphan.[36] God's perspective is dominantly relational, concerned with interactions between people and between them and God, while the world loves to reduce transactions to financial deals. The danger of the latter approach is that the needs of people, of real, live families, often get ignored or at least pushed way into the background.

Globalization is not all bad. The increase of trade between richer and poorer nations should, and does, lead to development in the poorer nations. It can give the less developed nations a world market for their products, and can provide employment and raised living standards. But dangers abound.[37] We live in what has been called a 20:80 world, where

The 20:80 world...

Industrialized countries

20% of world population

87% of world income

62% of global environmental 'footprint'

Rest of the world

80% of world population

13% of world income

38% of global environmental 'footprint'

20 percent of the world's population consumes 80 percent of the world's natural resources. The opening up of world markets by bodies such as the World Trade Organization (founded in 1995 to institutionalize the post-World War II General Agreement on Tariffs and Trade—GATT) has perpetuated world inequality by creating a climate that favors rich over poor countries. Though it has enabled the large transnational companies to move easily into less developed countries, often to the benefit of those countries, it also allows them to exit them readily when it is to

the economic advantage of the companies. That can have devastating social and economic consequences for the residents of those countries. The power of the rich trading countries to impose import barriers may also lead to increased inequity. For example, the import tariffs on agricultural products imposed by the European Union and the US cost developing countries an estimated $700 billion per year in lost revenues in 2000.

The Christian response to globalization needs to be deeper and more considered than a simple avowal that huge corporations are a bad thing. They may bring benefits globally by sharing technology and the fruits of resources to regions that otherwise would be far from them. But Christians can moderate the innate tendency of fallen humankind to self-profit at the expense of others by helping to put in place appropriate regulatory controls, and by shaming exploitative corporations into improved practices. In recent years, the exploitation of workers in poorer countries by some major western international companies—by paying below-living wages and employing child labor—has been effectively curbed by a large-scale show of public distaste at such practices. In a small way, the concern for ethical practice has led to the increase of partnerships between the high-income and low-income countries by setting up schemes such as the Fair Trade network and Traidcraft, which ensure good working practices in poorer countries. Although the prices of goods bought through such schemes may be somewhat higher than through mega-corporations, individuals are often willing to pay the extra based on their ethical convictions. Delivering a fair deal to subsistence farmers is certainly not a trivial exercise in an economic environment ruled by major international companies.

A further practical way in which Christians could live out such a "creation ethic" is by lobbying for proper account to be taken of the full cost of manufacturing goods that takes into account not only the marginal costs of such things as raw materials and salaries, but also of the environmental "capital" and human "capital" that is used. At present the economic system and pricing of consumer goods takes little account of the real cost of either the environmental impact of getting raw materials or of the human cost of the labor it utilizes. So the prices we pay for consumer goods do not factor in the long-term environmental or humanitarian costs of making and transporting those goods. For example, a major cause of global greenhouse gas emissions is the fuel burnt by aircraft and ships: if these fuels were taxed appropriately, it would change the economics of long-distance transport and probably reduce some of the unnecessary long-distance transportation with its associated pollution impacts. Until that is done properly, we are building and living off debt to future generations. It is striking that economists often talk almost entirely in "mechanical" terms, using words such as "inputs," "outputs," "levers" and "multipliers," whereas a more appropriate terminology often found in religious forums tends to use "organic" terms such as "seeds," "planting," "renewal" and "communities." In the long-term we need to move away from the ingrained concept in the high-income parts of the world of continual year-on-year growth: there is an illusion that this can be maintained by ever increasing technological sophistication, but there will always be a price to be paid for this, even if it comes at someone else's expense elsewhere in the world, or from future generations.

"Spaceship earth"

Viewed from space, the earth's biosphere—the part containing life—appears as a wafer-thin shell surrounding the solid earth. It extends through a thickness of only about fifty kilometers from the ocean floors, through the earth's surface and into the atmosphere. Though it has been the home of life for almost 4 billion years, from shortly after the earth's formation to the present day, it is a complex interdependent system. Just as on a closed spaceship, what we do in one part of the world cannot fail to affect other parts to a greater or lesser degree. Humankind's effect on the natural system is already immense. It is entirely possible that in a short space of time the influence of humans could so upset the ecological balance as to cause a catastrophic failure in some or many areas of the world. In our God-given role as stewards of God's created order, Christians should be at the forefront in helping to ensure that the resources of the world are used equitably, in a long-term sustainable manner, and with due regard to the impact of our activities both on other people around the globe and on future generations.[38]

CHAPTER 9

Christians in Science

In this book we have mapped out a relationship between science and faith that may surprise some people because they have been brought up to believe that science and faith are intrinsically antagonistic. But we have suggested that the reality is very different. The roots of the modern scientific movement are embedded in a Judeo-Christian worldview and this alone helps to explain many of the powerful affinities between science and Christian faith that endure to the present day.[1] Scientists and Christians share a mutual suspicion of the more extreme claims made by the postmodernist—that all truths are ultimately relative. Both the scientific and Christian enterprises share the conviction that there are certain principles built into the order of the universe that are true for all people in all cultures and contexts. And today Christians remain very active within the scientific community, lobbying for the most effective ways of applying science in technology, and determined to utilize the fruits of science for the benefit of humanity.

Such aspirations certainly sound lofty and worthy, but how in practice can they be worked out? In the hard-nosed, pragmatic environment of the scientific community, high-sounding goals are of little use unless they can be shown to be realistically achievable. In this final chapter we consider some of the practical outworkings of being a Christian in science.

Scientists in society

Among the characteristics of the scientific enterprise are its uniquely *international* nature, with a common shared methodology and much common terminology and language. Scientific advances invariably build upon a common pool of shared knowledge and understanding, which requires a high degree of cooperative endeavor. In an era characterized by the increasing fragmentation of cultures and the growth of nationalism based on ethnic, cultural and religious differences, the scientific community provides a powerful antidote. Though this is not driven by specifically Christian imperatives, it certainly is in keeping with the biblical injunctions to live in peace and love with our neighbors, and reflects God's opposition to the jealousies and selfishness which underpin strife between peoples.

From the earliest days of organized science, it has been an international activity. Indeed, even in the seventeenth century, individual scientists were in regular and rapid communication by letter with other colleagues abroad about their latest thoughts and discoveries. Nowadays, national scientific academies, such as the Royal Society in Great Britain and the National Academy of Sciences in the United States, allocate considerable sums of money specifically to facilitate international exchanges with scientists from other countries, to foster and support international conferences, and to encourage the publication of scientific results in publicly available international journals. The international, open nature of science remains one of its core values. Even throughout periods of international isolation between different nations, such as the Cold War of the late twentieth century, or the shunning of the apartheid government of South Africa from the 1950s to the 1980s, contacts frequently remained open at the level of working scientists.

The underlying quantitative nature of science, and the use of tools such as mathematics to build models of how the materials in the world behave, provide an international language that crosses cultural, social and national boundaries. As a cohesive force in a fragmented world, science therefore plays an important and positive role.

This is furthered by the cooperative nature of the scientific enterprise. Every scientist is heavily dependent on the work of others. Isaac Newton recognized this when he wrote in a letter to the scientist Robert Hooke: "If I have seen further, it is by standing on the shoulders of giants."[2] The interdependence and importance of the work of numerous different scientists, some famous, many others anonymous, in formulating our current scientific theories has strong resonances in the Christian view that everyone has equal importance before God, despite individuals having widely differing skills, gifts and abilities. As Paul wrote of the Christian community, "The body is a unit, though it is made up of many parts; and though all its parts are many, they form one body,"[3] a view which is sadly lacking in much contemporary culture.

Christians should be, and often are, at the forefront of promoting the international and cooperative nature of the scientific enterprise. Sometimes this may involve sacrificing a more successful scientific career in one country in order to move to another part of the world to help those less fortunate than ourselves. In fact, this is what one of us (DA) did in their own career—spending 15 years working in the Middle East to help in getting scientific research off the ground in different universities. This is definitely not a good move for building up the best publications record, but unless the command of Jesus to "love your neighbor as yourself" involves such career moves for at least some Christians, then the command has no teeth and remains mere words.

Science for the common good

We have already outlined in this book some of the ways in which science offers huge potential benefits in its ability to provide remedies for the afflictions facing humankind. An obvious example is in the advances in medical techniques, which have already produced a considerable extension in normal life expectancy, at least for those living in high-income countries. But the possibilities for improving the lot of humankind extend across all the sciences, including, for example: the development of tailored crop strains better suited to coping with climatic conditions and endemic diseases in different targeted parts of the world, which may therefore help alleviate the widespread specter of famine; ways of generating energy that will enable more of the world's population to have access to improved standards of living (and in many cases to raise them from the very lowest levels); care for the environment in ways that will prevent large segments of the present and future population becoming disadvantaged or even dispossessed of their land and livelihood by rapid climatic change or by the effects of pollution or other fallout from industrial activities; and so on—including advances that we cannot yet even imagine or anticipate.

Christians have an important part to play in ensuring that scientific advances are available for the common good. Human nature is such that people are only too willing to take advantage of circumstances that may enable them to push themselves ahead of others: and scientific knowledge can easily fall into this category, by providing small segments of society, or indeed of high-income nations as a whole, with considerable power over others who do not have that knowledge. For example, a long battle was fought over whether or not parts of the human genome sequence could be patented. The temptation for large privately funded research corporations to patent part of the human genome sequence was that if this turned out to contain the coding for some disease that could be treated by therapeutic genetic

modification, then that company, with its monopoly on the information, stood to make a lot of money from the patent. The vast majority
of scientists were opposed to such restrictions by patent on what is,
after all, a basic description of how we humans are made. And in the
event, although patent disputes on the matter are not yet over, the rapidity of publication of the human genome by publicly funded research bodies in the United Kingdom and United States, together with
eventual agreement, between the publicly and privately funded research institutes, meant that the information on the sequence of the
human genome has indeed been placed in the public domain.

Further along the line, when basic scientific research has been developed into usable technology, the issues of justice and accessibility to
the fruits of that technology by poorer segments of society become even
more pressing and personal. The availability of specialist drugs fall into
this category. A current example is the expensive drugs for treating
AIDS. The cost for drugs that people with AIDS in the US are willing
and able to pay is far higher than most of those in sub-Saharan Africa
could afford, even though the scale of the problem is much greater in Africa. The actual cost of manufacturing the drugs once they have been developed is relatively low. So there is a strong case to be made for making
such drugs available in Africa at lower cost than in the US. There is some
movement by the big pharmaceutical companies toward doing this, but
it is an area that requires continual vigilance to maintain a just distribution of the benefits of science.

There are, of course, good reasons for allowing some financial
protection for companies undertaking expensive research and development programs to bring scientific advances to the marketplace, and this
is a proper use of patent protection. But it is important to maintain a
balance between equitable rewards to encourage investment in high-
expense or high-risk technological development that otherwise would
not occur, and straight selfishness in preventing others from reaping any
of the fruits of particular technological developments. It is appropriate
that Christians should seek to ensure that such balances are maintained
equitably and with justice, and to seek to foster public debate to change
the status quo where they are not.

In the broader philosophical sphere, Christians can point to the
limitations as well as to the possibilities of science. In the mid-twentieth
century there was in many people's minds a view that science could ultimately answer all the woes of humankind—that someone, somewhere
would eventually find a technological fix for everything from aging
to atmospheric pollution, from cancer to car exhaust emissions, from
diabetes to deforestation. Though at the beginning of the twenty-first

century it is manifestly plain to most people that limitless technological advances do not solve all the problems of society at a stroke, there often remains an underlying sense that science ultimately ought to be able to explain everything, and to somehow make everything better. Christians who are scientists are perhaps the best placed of all to point out that science only deals with the material aspects of God's creation; that arguably the more important aspects of human life, of relationships with other people and with our creator God, are entirely outside the remit of science. And of course Christians will want to point out that many of the woes of humankind stem ultimately from the rebellion of humankind against our creator God and the resultant prevalence of evil in the world. They can go on to proclaim that the revelation of God through the written word in the Bible, and supremely through the life and death of God's son, Jesus, alone enable us to make sense of our place in this universe, and to bring us back into relationship with God. The ultimate answers to human dilemmas lie well beyond science.

At the other end of the spectrum, from those who think that making full use of human creativity and ingenuity in developing technological advances are a good thing, are those who suggest that "meddling with nature" is wrong. Scientists who are Christians will want to point out that if God is indeed the creator of this universe, and has put us in charge of creation to look after it properly, then we will want to fulfill that responsibility to the best of our abilities. If leaving nature as it is means that more people starve, more people die from preventable diseases and millions of people are forced to live in atrocious environments, then Christians would prefer to take action.

So for Christians it is our responsibility as stewards of God's creation to play our part in ensuring that the world is left as a fit place, and preferably as a better place, in which to live—for both our contemporaries and for future generations. Depending on our circumstances, we may only have influence over personal or local issues, or perhaps we may be able to influence global issues. Either way, the demands by God that we walk rightly and act justly are the same. And this responsibility is ours whether or not others around us acknowledge the lordship of Christ, and whether or not they are even aware of our actions.

The Christian ethic, with its strongly counter-cultural stance, is well placed to take the lead in promoting individual, societal and governmental policies and practices of sustainable consumption. It can do so from two powerful positions. First, the foundational Christian view is that this physical world is only a temporary residence for individuals in an eternal time frame. So although the way we use the material resources around us here on earth may have eternal consequences,[4] the possession or otherwise of strictly material possessions is not the main, or even an important, part of our life on earth. Indeed, Jesus made clear that the love of material possessions is actually a major impediment to our eternal well-being.[5] So there are strong reasons to limit our own use of resources. Second, it is a proper Christian responsibility to engage in science to push forward technological solutions to some of the inequities and hardships of living in this world. And throughout history Christians have often been in the forefront of such work.

Scientists as individuals

The standards of personal conduct, of ethical considerations, and of concern for others around them appropriate to Christians who are scientists are, of course, no different from those faced by Christians in other walks of life. But inevitably, pressure points may sometimes be different. While excessive money making as a priority may be generally a lesser temptation to the academic scientist than to the businessman, simply because the opportunity is not there, other temptations may be much more powerful. For example, the urge to push one's own reputation ahead of that of others, perhaps even to the extent of doing others down so that you yourself may seem to become more important, is endemic in academic scientific circles. One of the published tools of science are exhaustive tabulations showing how many times, and by whom, each of one's scientific publications have been referenced by others: these are perused avidly both by individual scientists and by funding and award-giving organizations, so the urge to find ways to enhance one's own reputation may be extremely strong.

Sometimes the argument is used that science is itself neutral and value-free: that if, say, an understanding of nuclear processes is used by a terrorist to make a nuclear bomb, then that is not the responsibility of the scientist who discovered radioactivity, or who worked on better theories of nuclear fission. It is certainly true that all the possible future uses of scientific research cannot possibly be foreseen, and indeed there may be unexpected uses of scientific knowledge for good as well as for evil. But there are some areas in which the scientist, with their technical understanding, cannot simply bury their head in the sand and claim that science is neutral and that what others do with it is not their responsibility. If the scientist who has the ability to understand complex new issues abrogates their responsibility to ensure that society deals with the issues in a way that is just and fair for others, then setting the agenda will be left to those who either do not understand the issues, or who have no qualms about acting irresponsibly or selfishly. Jesus had a lot to say about how we will be judged for the way we have used the gifts and abilities given to us,[6] and those Christians who are scientists need to take this seriously.

In the light of the Christian understanding that every single person is made in God's image, and is loved by God, one area where Christians should bring their influence to bear is in ensuring that both scientific research itself, and also the potential applications of that research, respect the rights and dignity of other people. Although it is undoubtedly easier in the short term to keep one's head well below the laboratory bench over contentious issues, and to excuse oneself with the argument that the science itself is value-free, this hardly seems to fulfil Jesus' mandate for Christians to be "salt of the world," even though it may be unpopular and costly to do so.[7] This may well mean lobbying or using other avenues available to make sure that legislation is put in place to prevent abuses of scientific knowledge or research.

It is a truism that once something appears to be possible, someone, somewhere will want to do it. And some scientists may well take the line, "Why not? Let's try it and see what happens." An example might be the issue of human cloning. The Christian would want to say that we need to put limits on what is allowed simply in order to respect the sanctity and dignity of human life, and that for this reason, even were it possible, we should still want to maintain the present illegality of the reproductive cloning of humans.

The Christian also brings a realistic perspective of the nature of human behavior, and in particular of the innate tendency of people toward sinful behavior. So in that respect the Christian should be able to bring a balance to legislation that recognizes the optimism and potential of new scientific research and methods, while being aware of the realistic dangers inherent in scientific research if society places no restrictions on what is permissible.

Another area where Christians can make a practical difference in science is by maintaining the highest standards of integrity in the way that scientific results are obtained and reported. This involves acknowledging the intellectual and experimental input of all those, without exception, who have contributed to a particular project. It means being willing to be a "whistle-blower" (often at considerable cost to a scientific career), if one becomes aware that colleagues are reporting their results in a fraudulent manner. And of course it means being rigorous about the assessment and presentation of one's own results when writing scientific papers. If truth-telling in the scientific community is undermined, then the whole scientific enterprise is called into question.

Perhaps above all the Christian has the privilege of seeing their scientific research as part of their worship, as Francis Collins has so eloquently described it (see p. 66). This gives a whole new dimension and "buzz" to their research activities. Whereas the non-Christian will see the scientific breakthrough as a matter of personal pride and achievement—and there is certainly nothing wrong with that—the Christian has the additional joy of knowing that they are glorifying God by understanding the universe just that little bit better.

So to finish on a personal note, we are both immensely grateful for the sheer fun of being able to study a created world that reflects God's plans and actions. Amongst all the often tedious leg work, report writing, organizing, fund raising and blind alleys that are an inevitable part of contemporary scientific research, the unexpected joy of suddenly understanding some small corner of God's world better is hard to beat. It provides a deep reminder that we ourselves are part of that created order and that, in God's goodness, God allows us to participate in that creation. And, if we choose to do so, to align ourselves to God's will in using our discoveries to serve others.

Endnotes

NOTES FOR CHAPTER 1: WHAT'S IT ALL ABOUT?

1. J. D. Watson and F. H. C. Crick, "A structure for deoxyribose nucleic acid," *Nature* 71, 1953, pp. 737–38.

2. See, for example, the articles "Sitting in judgment," *Nature* 419, 2002, pp. 332–33; and "Paper retracted as co-author admits forgery," *Nature* 421, 2003, p. 775.

3. A readable discussion of positivism and of other philosophical standpoints in the scientific enterprise is given by D. Ratzsch in *Science and its Limits: The Natural Sciences in Christian Perspective,* Leicester: InterVarsity Press, 2000.

4. K. Popper, cited in D. R. Alexander, *Beyond Science,* Tring: Lion Publishing, 1972, p. 73.

NOTES FOR CHAPTER 2: KNOWLEDGE—SCIENTIFIC AND RELIGIOUS

1. This theme is developed in greater depth by M. C. Banner in *The Justification of Science and the Rationality of Religious Belief,* Oxford: Clarendon Press, 1990. See also R. O'Connor, "Criteria of success in science and theology," *Science & Christian Belief* 10, 1998, pp. 21–40, and P. Dowe, "Response to O'Connor: inference to the best explanation and predictive power," *Science & Christian Belief* 10, 1998, pp. 41–47.

2. 1 Corinthians 15:17.

3. T. Kuhn, *The Structure of Scientific Revolutions,* Chicago: University of Chicago Press, 1962.

4. An example of this latter group might be W. B. Drees, *Religion, Science and Naturalism,* Cambridge: Cambridge University Press, 1996.

5. R. Dawkins, *The Ultraviolet Garden,* Royal Institution Christmas Lecture, No 4, 1991.

6. See F. M. Turner "The Victorian conflict between science and religion: a professional dimension," *Isis* 69, 1978, pp. 356–76; J. H. Brooke, *Science and Religion: Some Historical Perspectives,* Cambridge: Cambridge University Press, 1991; Denis Alexander, *Rebuilding the Matrix: Science and Faith in the 21st Century,* Oxford: Lion Publishing, 2001.

7. C. A. Russell "The conflict metaphor and its social origins," *Science & Christian Belief* 1, 1989, pp. 3–26.

8. F. J. Tipler, *The Physics of Eternity: Modern Cosmology, God, and the Resurrection of the Dead,* Doubleday, 1994. For a critique of Tipler's position see W. R. Stoeger and G. F. R. Ellis, "A response to Tipler's Omega-Point theory," *Science & Christian Belief* 7, 1995, pp. 163–72.

9. F. Bacon (1605) *The Advancement of Learning, 1.6.16,* quoted by Norma Emerton in "The argument from design in early modern natural theology," *Science & Christian Belief* 1, 1989, pp. 129–47.

10. Something rather like this stance was taken by S. J. Gould in "Nonoverlapping Magisteria," *Natural History* 106, March 1997, pp. 16–22; reprinted in *Leonardo's Mountain of Clams and the Diet of Worms,* New York: Harmony Books, 1998, pp. 269–83. But on the other hand many of Gould's writings on the history of science illustrate the rich and positive interactions between science and faith, so Gould did not practice his "NOMA" principle as rigorously as this article might suggest.

11. See, for example, J. H. Brooke, *Science and Religion: Some Historical Perspectives,* Cambridge: Cambridge University Press, 1991.

12. M. Poole, *A Guide to Science and Christian Belief,* Oxford: Lion Publishing, 1994.

13. R. J. Berry, *Real Science, Real Faith,* Eastbourne: Monarch, 1991, reprinted 1995.

14. E. J. Larson and L. Witham, "Scientists are still keeping the faith," *Nature* 386, 1997, 435–36.

NOTES FOR CHAPTER 3: IS SCIENCE DISCREDITED?

1. C. A. Russell, *Cross-currents: Interactions between Science and Faith.* Leicester: InterVarsity Press, 1985, p. 195.

2. P. Teilhard de Chardin *The Phenomenon of Man,* London: Collins, 1959, p. 288. Although written in manuscript form in 1938, his Jesuit superiors forbade him from publishing, and it was only after his death that his friends were able to publish his work, since permission from his church superiors to publish was only required for the work of a living writer.

3. See, for example, a critique by M. Schluter and D. Lee, *The R Factor,* London: Hodder & Stoughton, 1993, of the way in which the de-

velopment of public policies and a highly mobile workforce has led to the erosion of relationships between individuals, both within families and in the wider social, business and economic contexts. Christianity is rooted in relationships, with the first two commandments focusing on love for God and love for our neighbor, so erosion of relationships can only move society further from God's ways. The Relationships Foundation (3 Hooper Street, Cambridge CB1 2NZ, UK) is seeking to develop practical ways of approaching political, social and economic reform using a relational approach, which, although founded on the ethical values of the Judeo-Christian tradition, does not require any theological beliefs of its supporters.

4. As an example of the reluctance of the US Senate to reduce greenhouse gas emissions, a resolution prior to the 1997 Kyoto environmental summit proposing that the US should not agree to limit emissions unless developing countries also adopted binding targets, was carried by a 95–0 vote. This despite the fact that the US is by far the most energy intensive nation per capita in the world, and is a nation where emissions could readily be reduced. And in 2001, shortly after his election as president of the United States, George W. Bush, withdrew the US from commitments made by his predecessor to greenhouse gas emission controls, saying that he would not consent to anything that might damage the economic well-being of his own country.

5. National Science Board (2000) Science and Engineering Indicators—2000. Washington, US Government Printing Office.

6. John D Miller (2000) Public understanding of, and attitudes toward, scientific research: what we know and what we need to know, *Public Understanding of Science,* vol. 13, pp. 273–94.

7. R. Parsons (ed.), *Revision Guide for GCSE Double Science, Physics,* Kirby-in-Furness, Cumbria: The Science Coordination Group, 1998.

8. L. Wolpert, *The Unnatural Nature of Science.* London: Faber, 1992.

9. Jacques Hadamard, *The Psychology of Invention in the Mathematical Field,* Princeton: Princeton University Press, 1949. See also chapter 4 on "Creativity" in L. Wolpert, *The Unnatural Nature of Science,* London: Faber, 1992.

10. 1 Corinthians 15:14.

11. John L. Taylor, "The postmodern attack on scientific realism," *Science & Christian Belief* 14, 2002, pp. 99–106.

12. Genesis 1:31.

13. W. Buckland, *Geology and Mineralogy Considered with Reference to Natural Theology, Treatise VI (Vol. 1),* The Bridgewater Treatises,

in two volumes. (F. T. Buckland, ed.), New York: George Routledge & Co., 1858, p. 9.

14. B. Ramm, *The Christian View of Science and Scripture,* Grand Rapids, Michigan, US: Eerdmans Publishing Co., 1954, p. 25.

15. The council of The Royal Society issued a statement in 1998 supporting the view that "reproductive cloning of humans to term by nuclear substitution is morally and ethically unacceptable and believe it should be prohibited" (R. B. Heap and others, *Whither Cloning?* London: The Royal Society). The European Parliament also passed a resolution on cloning in 1997 asserting that "the cloning of human beings . . . cannot under any circumstances be justified or tolerated by any society . . . and human cloning is, and must continue to be, prohibited." See Chapter 7 for a further discussion of this topic.

16. A good account of New Age thinking and its relation to science and to Christianity is given by Ernest Lucas, *Science and the New Age Challenge,* Leicester: Apollos, 1996.

17. Kepler's prayer is quoted in a footnote by W. Buckland, *Geology and Mineralogy Considered with Reference to Natural Theology, Treatise VI (Vol. 1),* The Bridgewater Treatises (F. T. Buckland, ed.), New York: George Routledge & Co., 1858, p. 9, from a translated version published in the *Christian Observer,* August 1834, p. 495.

NOTES FOR CHAPTER 4: IS RELIGION DISCREDITED?

1. Romans 8:28.

2. Philippians 4:11, 12.

3. S. W. Hawking, *A Brief History of Time,* London: Bantam, 1988. See also D. Wilkinson, *God, the Big Bang and Stephen Hawking,* Tunbridge Wells: Monarch, 1998, for a sensitive and helpful account of the contributions made by Professor Stephen Hawking to understanding the early origins of the universe, and issues of how to relate science and religion, particularly in the area of astronomy.

4. R. Dawkins, *The Blind Watchmaker,* Harlow: Longman, 1986.

5. For a discussion of Dawkins' views from a Christian perspective, see M. Poole, "A critique of aspects of the philosophy and theology of Richard Dawkins," *Science & Christian Belief* 6, 1994, pp. 41–59, and the subsequent exchange of comments by Dawkins and Poole, *Science & Christian Belief* 7, 1995, pp. 45–58.

6. MacKay coined the phrase "nothing buttery" in a 1960 article entitled "Man as a mechanism," *Faith and Thought* 91, p. 149. It was expanded in his 1974 book *The Clockwork Image,* London: InterVarsity Press, pp. 21, 40–45.

7. Quoted by M. Poole, "A critique of aspects of the philosophy and theology of Richard Dawkins," *Science & Christian Belief* 6, 1994, pp. 41–59.

8. A helpful and readable review of New Age thinking, on which this summary draws, is given by E. Lucas *Science and the New Age Challenge*, Leicester: Apollos, 1996.

9. This description of the New Age is given by D. Groothuis, quoted by M. Cole et al., *What is the New Age?* London: Hodder & Stoughton, 1990, p. 6.

10. E. Miller, *A Crash Course on the New Age Movement*, Eastbourne: Monarch, 1990.

11. C. Riddell, *The Findhorn Community*, Forres: Findhorn Press, 1990, p. 30.

12. G. Zukav, *The Dancing Wu Li Masters*, London: Flamingo, 1989, p. 331.

13. E. Lucas, *Science and the New Age Challenge*, Leicester: Apollos, 1996. p. 30.

14. F. Capra, *The Tao of Physics*, London: Flamingo, 1983.

15. G. Zukav, *The Dancing Wu Li Masters*, London: Flamingo, 1989, p. 177.

16. S. MacLaine, *Dancing in the Light*, New York: Bantam, 1986, p. 337.

17. R. K. Clifton and M. G. Regehr, "Capra on eastern mysticism and modern physics: a critique," *Science & Christian Belief* 1, 1989, pp. 53–74.

18. See Psalm 19:1 and Romans 1:19, 20.

19. See N. Emerton, "The Argument from Design," *Science & Christian Belief* 1, 1989, pp. 129–47; C. A. Russell, *Cross-currents: Interactions between Science and Faith*, Leicester: InterVarsity Press, 1985, p. 111; D. A. Wilkinson, "The revival of natural theology in contemporary cosmology," *Science & Christian Belief*, 2, 1990, pp. 95–115.

20. J. Dillenberger, *Protestant Thought and Natural Science*, London: Collins, 1961, pp. 133–90.

21. Acts 17:22–29.

22. Romans 1:20.

23. Acts 14:11.

24. Psalm 19:1.

25. R. Dawkins, *The Blind Watchmaker*, Harlow: Longman, 1986.

26. S. W. Hawking, *A Brief History of Time*, London: Bantam, 1988, p. 141.

27. See the lecture by John Polkinghorne entitled "Has science made religion redundant?" at www.st-edmunds.cam.ac.uk/cis/polkinghorne.

28. Denis Alexander, *Rebuilding the Matrix: Science and Faith in the 21st Century,* Lion Publishing: Oxford, 2001, see especially Chapter 12.

29. Isaiah 45:7.

30. Matthew 5:45.

31. Matthew 6:26.

32. Matthew 6:30.

33. Colossians 1:16, 17.

34. Hebrews 1:3.

35. John 1:1–10.

36. E.g., see Simon Conway Morris, *Life's Solution,* Cambridge: Cambridge University Press, 2003, Chapter 4 "The origin of life: straining the soup or our credulity?"

37. A. Moore, *Science and Faith,* London: Kegan Paul, Trench & Co, 1989, p. 184.

38. Narnia is the mythical land ruled by Aslan, described by C. S. Lewis in his enduring allegory of the forces of good and evil in his Narnia series of books.

NOTES FOR CHAPTER 5: SCIENCE ENCOUNTERS FAITH

1. Isaiah 46:10.

2. Space does not allow consideration of this historical claim further here, but see: R. Hooykaas, *Religion and the Rise of Modern Science,* Edinburgh: Scottish Academic Press, 1972; C. A. Russell, *Cross-Currents: Interactions Between Science and Faith,* Leicester: InterVarsity Press, 1985; D. C. Lindberg and R. L. Numbers (eds.), *God and Nature: Historical Essays on the Encounter Between Christianity and Science,* University of California Press, 1986; J. H. Brooke, *Science and Religion: Some Historical Perspectives,* Cambridge: Cambridge University Press, 1991; P. Harrison, *The Bible, Protestantism and the Rise of Natural Science,* Cambridge: Cambridge University Press, 1998; J. Brooke and G. Cantor, *Reconstructing Nature: The Engagement of Science and Religion,* Edinburgh: T&T Clark, 1998; D. R. Alexander, *Rebuilding the Matrix: Science and Faith in the 21st Century,* Oxford: Lion, 2001.

3. Personal communication.

4. F. Bacon, *The New Atlantis,* vol. III, Part 2, The Harvard Classics, New York: P. F. Collier and Son, 1909–14; Bartleby.com, 2001.

5. For a helpful discussion of how scientists often accommodate observations that apparently don't fit any of the extant theories, without breaking their faith in the correctness or usefulness of the main theories themselves, see D. Ratzsch, *Science and Its Limits,* Leicester: InterVarsity Press, 2000.

6. See C. Humphreys, *The Miracles of Exodus: A Scientist's Discovery of the Extraordinary Natural Causes of the Biblical Stories,* London: Continuum, 2003, for a discussion of likely explanations of the miraculous occurrences recorded during that period. Note that Colin Humphreys himself is emphatic that "a natural explanation of the events of the Exodus doesn't to my mind make them any less miraculous . . . the ancient Israelite believed that their God worked in, with, and through natural events. What made certain natural events miraculous was their timing" (p. 5).

7. This story is recorded in John 11:1–44.

8. An excellent and highly readable account of Galileo's life and of his trial for heresy, from which this quotation is taken, is given by D. Sobel, *Galileo's Daughter,* London: Penguin Books, 1999, using extant letters written to Galileo by his daughter, who was a cloistered nun.

9. See http://map.gsfc.nasa.gov/m_mm/mr_age.html for details of the age of the universe deduced from cosmic background radiation. Full technical details are in C. L. Bennett et al., "First year Wilkinson Microwave Anisotropy Probe (WMAP) observations: preliminary maps and basic results," *Astrophysical Journal Supplement,* 148, 2003, pp. 1–28.

10. C.J. Allègre, G. Manhès and C. Göpel, "The age of the earth," *Geochimica Cosmochimica Acta* 59, 1995, pp. 1445–56.

11. A. N. Halliday, "Terrestrial accretion rates and the origin of the moon," *Earth and Planetary Science Letters* 176, 2000, pp. 17–30.

12. S. A. Wilde, J. W. Valley, W. H. Peck and C. M. Graham, "Evidence from detrital zircons for the existence of continental crust and oceans on the earth 4.4 Gys ago," *Nature* 409, 2001, pp. 175–78.

13. R. A. Stern and W. Blecker, "Age of the world's oldest rocks refined using Canada's SHRIMP: the Acasta Greiss Complex, Northwest Territories, Canada," *Geosciences Canada* 25–1, 1998, pp. 27–31.

14. A. J. Mojzsis, G. Arrhenius, K. D. McKeegan, T. M. Harrison, A. P. Nutman and C. R. L. Friend, "Evidence for life on earth before 3,800 million years ago," *Nature* 384, 1996, pp. 55–59.

15. E. G. Nisbet and N. H. Sleep, "The habitat and nature of early life," *Nature* 409, 2001, pp. 1083–91.

16. G. M. Narbonne and J. G. Gehling "Life after snowball: the oldest complex Ediacaran fossils," *Geology* 31, 2003, pp. 27–30.

17. Q. Ji, Z.-X. Luo, C.-X. Yuan, J. R. Wible, J.-P. Zhang and J. A. Georgi, "The earliest known eutherian mammal," *Nature* 416, 2002, pp. 816–22. Eomaia ("Dawn Mother") is a small creature about the size of a large mouse, with exceptionally well preserved skeleton, teeth, foot bones, cartilages and fur found in the Yixian Formation of Liaoning

Province, China. It is the oldest known representative of the lineage leading to placental mammals, including humans.

18. S. Jones, R. Martin and D. Pilbeam (eds), *The Cambridge Encyclopedia of Human Evolution,* Cambridge: Cambridge University Press, 1992.

19. T. D. White, B. Asfaw, D. Degusta, H. Gilbert, G. D. Richards, G. Suwa and F. C. Howell, "Pleistocene *Homo sapiens* from Middle Awash, Ethiopia," *Nature* 423, 2003, pp. 742–47.

20. C. Humphreys, "The star of Bethlehem," *Science & Christian Belief* 5, 1993, pp. 83–101. Note that the date of the birth of Jesus is B.C.E. because the Julian calendar in use today assumed an incorrect year for the birth of Christ (and also neglected to insert a year 0 between 1 B.C.E. and 1 C.E.).

21. C. Humphreys and W. G. Waddington, "Dating the crucifixion," *Nature* 306, 1983, pp. 743–46.

22. M. Rees, *Our Final Century: Terror, Error or Environmental Disaster,* Random House, 2003.

23. Matthew 10:29.

24. Sir John Houghton, who has worked extensively with the Intergovernmental Panel on Climate Change, develops the idea of stewardship in terms of being gardeners of God's earth in Chapter 8 of his book *Global Warming: the Complete Briefing,* Cambridge: Cambridge University Press, 1997.

25. Genesis 11:9 describes the dispersion of people and the start of their diverse languages.

NOTES FOR CHAPTER 6: CREATED OR EVOLVED?

1. Parts of this section are based on a lecture given by Denis Alexander on 2 March 1998, at Trinity College, Cambridge, entitled "Does evolution have any religious significance?," published by Christians in Science (see http://www.cis.org.uk). It is also available for download for free from the Christians in Science website (http://www.cis.org.uk/articles/evolution_relig_signif/alexander_01.htm) where other similar material is often posted. The lecture considers some other questions raised about evolution which space does not permit us to consider in detail here, such as human evolution, the Fall, and the question of death, pain and suffering. See also R. J. Berry, *God and The Biologist,* Leicester: Apollos, 1996; E. Lucas, *Genesis Today—Genesis and the Questions of Science,* Christian Impact, Vere Street, London W1M 9HP, 1995 (in case of difficulty either book can be obtained from Christians in Science). Also

D. Alexander *Rebuilding the Matrix: Science and Faith in the 21st Century,* Oxford: Lion Publishing, 2001, has several chapters on evolution.

2. The details are in D. C. Lindberg and R. L. Numbers (eds), *God and Nature: Historical Essays on the Encounter Between Christianity and Science,* University of California Press, 1986, pp. 407–15; R. L. Numbers, *The Creationists,* University of California Press, 1992.

3. Quoted by P. Kitcher, *Abusing Science,* Open University Press, 1983, p. 187.

4. P. E. Johnson, *Testing Darwinism,* 1997, InterVarsity Press.

5. M. A. F. Noor, "Genes to make new species," *Nature* 423, 2003, pp. 699–700.

6. P. Skelton (ed.), *Evolution,* Addison-Wesley Publishing, 1993, pp. 402–408. See also the example of speciation in the Hawaiian drosophilids in this chapter.

7. E. Verheyan et al., "Origin of the superflock of cichlid fishes from Lake Victoria, East Africa," *Science* 300, 2003, pp. 325–29.

8. J. Zhang, "Evolution by gene duplication: an update," *Trends in Ecology and Evolution* 18, 2003, pp. 292–98.

9. W. H. Li, "Evolutionary analyses of the human genome," *Nature* 409, 2001, pp. 847–49.

10. L. W. Hiller et al., "The DNA sequence of human chromosome 7," *Nature* 424, 2003, pp. 157–64.

11. M. Levine and R. Tjian, "Transcription regulation and animal diversity," *Nature* 424, 2003, pp 147–51.

12. S. B. Carroll, "Genetics and the making of *Homo sapiens,*" *Nature* 422, 2003, pp. 849–57.

13. Those interested in human evolution will enjoy: G. Finlay, "Homo divinus: the ape that bears God's image," *Science & Christian Belief* 15, 2003, pp. 17–40.

14. Psalm 104:30.

15. Isaiah 45:7.

16. J. R. Moore, *The Post-Darwinian Controversies,* Cambridge: Cambridge University Press, 1979, p. 92.

17. G. M. Marsden, *Science and Creationism* (ed. A. Montagu), Oxford: Oxford University Press (OUP), 1984, p. 101.

18. See D. N. Livingstone, *Darwin's Forgotten Defenders: Encounter Between Evangelical Theology and Evolutionary Thought,* Edinburgh: Scottish Academic Press, 1987.

19. 1 Kings 22:15–28.

20. 1 Kings 22:34.

21. M. J. Behe, *Darwin's Black Box: The Biochemical Challenge to Evolution,* New York: Free Press, 1996.

22. W. A. Dembski, *"The Design Inference: Eliminating Chance Through Small Probabilities,"* Cambridge: Cambridge University Press, 1998.

23. See also W. A. Dembski, *No Free Lunch: Why Specified Complexity Cannot Be Purchased Without Intelligence,* Lanham, Md.: Rowman & Littlefield Publishers, 2002. Also see a more detailed critique of Dembski's ideas in H. Van Till, "Are bacterial flagella intelligently designed? Reflections on the rhetoric of the modern ID movement," *Science & Christian Belief* 15, 2003, pp. 117–40.

24. X. Xu and R. F. Doolittle "Presence of a vertebrate fibrinogen-like sequence in an echinoderm," *Proceedings of the National Academy of Sciences US* 87, 1990, pp. 2097–101.

25. C. J. Jeffery (1999), "Moonlighting proteins," *Trends in Biochemical Sciences* 24, 1999, pp. 8–11.

26. Y. Jiang and R. F. Doolittle, "The evolution of vertebrate blood coagulation as viewed from a comparison of puffer fish and sea squirt genomes," *Proceedings of the National Academy of Sciences US* 100, 2003, pp. 7527–32.

27. For a critique of Behe's claims about cilia, see K. R. Miller, *Finding Darwin's God,* Harper Collins, 1999, pp. 140–43; and H. Van Till "Are bacterial flagella intelligently designed? Reflections on the rhetoric of the modern ID movement," *Science & Christian Belief* 15, 2003, pp. 117–40.

28. Psalm 19:1–6.

NOTES FOR CHAPTER 7: GENETICS AND SEX

1. See www.eugenicsarchive.org for sobering archival material from the American eugenics research 1910–40. Much of it was pervaded by prejudice against racial, ethnic and disabled groups.

2. F. S. Collins in the Foreword to T. Peters, *Playing God? Genetic Determinism and Human Freedom,* Routledge, 1997, pp. x–xi.

3. Acts 3:15; John 1:3.

4. Genesis 1:26–27.

5. Genesis 1:26–28 and 2:15; Psalm 24:1.

6. Genesis 3:16–19.

7. Romans 8:22 and 8:19, respectively.

8. Revelation 21:1.

9. Cited in M. J. Reiss and R. Straughan, *Improving Nature? The Science and Ethics of Genetic Engineering,* Cambridge: Cambridge University Press, 1996.

10. R. Hooykaas, *Religion and the Rise of Modern Science,* Edinburgh: Scottish Academic Press, 1972.

11. Genesis 1:28, 30; 2:15–20.

12. Genesis 9:1–3.

13. D. M. MacKay, *The Open Mind and Other Essays,* InterVarsity Press, 1988.

14. J. N. Perry, "Genetically modified crops," *Science & Christian Belief* 15, 2003, pp. 141–64.

15. G. Conway, "Regenerating the Green Revolution," in *GMOs: Ecological Dimensions.* Proceedings of the meeting 9–11 September 2002 at the University of Reading. Wellesbourne: Association of Applied Biologists.

16. For example, Amos 5:11–15; Zechariah 7:9–10; Jeremiah 22:16.

17. Isaiah 58:6–11.

18. The information in this paragraph is based on Ref. 14.

19. M. Qaim and D. Zilberman, "Yield effects of genetically modified crops in developing countries," *Science* 299, 2003, pp. 900–902.

20. *New Internationalist* 353, 2003, p. 20.

21. Y. Verlinsky et al., *Journal of the American Medical Association* 285, 2001, pp. 3130–33.

22. J. Savelescu, "Education and debate: deaf lesbians, 'designer disability,' and the future of medicine," *British Medical Journal* 325, 2002, pp. 771–73.

23. C. Dennis, "Synthetic sex cells," *Nature* 424, 2003, pp. 364–66.

24. See *Genetic Screening: Ethical Issues,* Nuffield Council on Bioethics, London, 1993. Also P. R. Reilly et al. *Nature Genetics* 15, 1997, pp. 16–20.

25. Report by the Human Genetics Commission, "Genes direct—ensuring the effective oversight of genetic tests supplied directly to the public," Department of Health, PO Box 777, London, SE1 6XH, UK, 2003. See http://www.hgc.gov.uk/genesdirect/.

26. This complex issue is helpfully discussed in *Human Genetics: Uncertainties and the Financial Implications Ahead,* a booklet obtainable from The Royal Society, 6 Carlton Terrace, London, SW1Y 5AG, UK.

27. D. B. Kohn, M. Sadelain and J. C. Glorioso, "Occurrence of leukaemia following gene therapy of X-linked SCID," *Nature Reviews Cancer* 3, 2003, pp. 477–88.

28. Genesis 11:1–9.

29. This section is based on a Cambridge Paper by D. Alexander called "Cloning Humans: Distorting the Image of God?," *The Cambridge Papers* Vol. 10, No. 2, June 2001. *The Cambridge Papers* are published four times per year and papers can be obtained by contacting the Jubilee

Centre at e-mail: jubilee.centre@clara.net. See also their website at http://www.jubilee-centre.org.

30. C. Simerly et al., "Molecular correlates of primate nuclear transfer failures," *Science* 300, 2003, p. 297.

31. K. Hochedlinger and R. Jaenisch, "Nuclear transplantation, embryonic stem cells, and the potential for cell therapy," *New England Journal of Medicine* 349, 2003, pp. 275–86.

32. I. Wilmut, K. Campbell and C. Tudge, *The Second Creation,* Headline, 2000.

33. See Genesis 1:27, 5:2 and 9:6–7.

34. See C. Ash, *Marriage: Sex in the Service of God,* InterVarsity Press, 2003.

35. M. Phippen, personal communication.

36. K. Hochedlinger and R. Jaenisch, "Nuclear transplantation, embryonic stem cells, and the potential for cell therapy," *New England Journal of Medicine* 349, 2003, pp. 275–86.

37. See M. May's own account of his experiences at http://www.senderogroup.com/perception.htm.

38. C. V. Joshi and T. Enver, "Plasticity revisited," *Current Opinion in Cell Biology* 14, 2002, pp. 749–55.

39. Y. Jiang et al., "Pluripotency of mesenchymal stem cells derived from adult marrow," *Nature* 418, 2002, pp. 41–49.

40. I. Kuehnle and M. A. Goodell, "The therapeutic potential of stem cells from adults," *British Medical Journal* 325, 2002, pp. 372–76.

41. Pontifical Academy for Life, "The Holy See, Declaration of Pontifical Academy for Life," in: Opinion No. 15 of the European Group on Ethics in Science and New Technologies to the European Commission. Ethical Aspects of Human Stem Cell Research and Use, Brussels, 14 November 2000, pp. 156–61.

42. The broad range of European views are reviewed in I. Nippert (2002) The pros and cons of human therapeutic cloning in the public debate, *Journal of Biotechnology* 98, 53–60. See also in the same Issue M. J. Reiss (2002) Ethical dimensions of therapeutic human cloning, *Journal of Biotechnology* 98, 61–70. A range of diverse US perspectives are given in I. L.Weissman (2002), "Human embryonic stem cells in science and medicine," *New England Journal of Medicine* 346, 1577–79, and in the letters published in response in *New England Journal of Medicine* (2002) 347, 1619–22.

43. D. Gareth Jones, "The human embryo: between oblivion and meaningful life," *Science & Christian Belief* 6, 1994, pp. 3–19; D. Gareth Jones, *Manufacturing Humans: The Challenge of the New Reproductive*

Technologies, InterVarsity Press, 1987; D. Gareth Jones, *Brave New People: Ethical Issues at the Commencement of Life,* InterVarsity Press, 1984.

44. M. J. Lysaght and A. L. Hazlehurst, "Private sector development of stem cell technology and therapeutic cloning," *Tissue Engineering* 9, 2003, pp. 555–61.

NOTES FOR CHAPTER 8: SPACESHIP EARTH

1. See Psalm 24:1; Revelation 4:11; Job 38:2–6.

2. See Oliver O'Donovan, *Resurrection and Moral Order: An Outline for Evangelical Ethics,* Leicester: InterVarsity Press, 1986, for a development of the argument that our present-day ethics should be founded and rooted in the Christian belief in the resurrection.

3. Revelation 21:1.

4. Revelation 21:4.

5. Isaiah 65:17; 66:22.

6. Romans 8:21; Hebrews 2:5–18; 2 Peter 3:13.

7. N. T. Wright, *New Heavens, New Earth: The Biblical Picture of the Christian Hope,* Grove Books Limited, Ridley Hall, Cambridge, 1999.

8. 1 Peter 1:4–5; 1 Corinthians 13:12.

9. 1 Corinthians 3:12–15.

10. See Luke 19:11–19.

11. Revelation 21:26.

12. Luke 24:13–31.

13. Accounts of the appearance of Jesus to the disciples in locked rooms shortly after his resurrection are given by Luke 24:36–43; John 20:19–20; John 20:26–28.

14. S. W. Hawking, *A Brief History of Time,* London: Bantam,1988.

15. Genesis 1:26–2:25.

16. Genesis 3:17–19.

17. J. Calvin, *Commentary on Genesis.* First Latin edition 1554. First English Edition 1578. Present translation 1847, reprinted by Banner of Truth publishers 1965.

18. Details are from R. L. Hooke, "On the history of humans as geomorphic agents," *Geology* 28, 2000, pp. 843–46.

19. See J. D. Milliman and J. P. M. Synitski, "Geomorphic/tectonic control of sediment discharge to the ocean: the importance of small mountain rivers," *Journal of Geology* 100, 1992, pp. 525–44.

20. An excellent summary of this work by the Intergovernmental Panel on Climate Change is given in *Climate Change 2001: The Scientific Basis,* 2001, available from the IPCC Secretariat, c/o World Meteorologi-

cal Organization, 7 bis Avenue de la Paix, Case Postale 2300, 1211 Geneva 2, Switzerland, and on the web at http://www.ipcc.ch. It is an outstanding example of an international group of scientific experts from the whole range of ethnic, cultural and religious backgrounds coming together to address a difficult and uncertain, but nevertheless crucial, global problem of relevance to the whole of mankind.

21. For a map of Bangladesh and for further details, see J. Houghton, *Global Warming: the Complete Briefing*. Cambridge: Cambridge University Press, 1997.

22. The Netherlands, for example, could protect against a 1 meter rise in sea level by spending an estimated $10,000 million: see J. G. de Ronde, "What will happen to the Netherlands if sea-level rise accelerates?" in *Climate and Sea-level Change: Observations, Projections and Implications*, R. A. Warrick, E. M. Barrow and T. M. L. Wigley (eds), Cambridge: Cambridge University Press, 1993, pp. 322–35.

23. See N. Myers and J. Kent, *Environmental Exodus: An Emergent Crisis in the Global Arena*, Washington, D.C., US: Climate Institute, 1995.

24. See also J. P. Burnside, *The Status and Welfare of Immigrants: The Place of the Foreigner in Biblical Laws and its Relevance to Contemporary Society*, Cambridge: The Jubilee Centre, 2001.

25. For a wider discussion of this issue, including helpful Christian perspectives, see the lecture and discussion on *Global Warming: the Science, the Impacts & the Politics*, published online at http://www.st-edmunds.cam.ac.uk/cis/houghton/index.html as part of a series by Christians in Science/Templeton Foundation.

26. Luke 12:48.

27. Matthew 10:16.

28. C. Hancock, "The 'Shrimp' who stopped slavery," *Christian History Magazine*, Issue 53, vol. 16, 1977, p. 12.

29. J. Houghton, *Global Warming: the Complete Briefing*, Cambridge: Cambridge University Press, 1997.

30. Sir John Houghton, who has worked extensively with the Intergovernmental Panel on Climate Change, develops the idea of stewardship in terms of being gardeners of God's earth in Chapter 8 of his book *Global Warming: The Complete Briefing*, 1997, op cit.

31. Genesis 11:9 describes the dispersion of people and the start of their diverse languages.

32. See the description of the regulations for the year of Jubilee, and God's reasons for them, in Leviticus 25:8–54.

33. See, for example, Matthew 19:16–24 for this story.

34. Genesis 3:17–19 reports the curse that God placed on the land as a result of Adam's disobedience to God.

35. A good source of these statistics is the website of the Food and Agriculture Organization of the United Nations at http://www.fao.org.

36. Leviticus 25:10; Deuteronomy 15; Nehemiah 10:31.

37. See P. S. Heslam, *Globalization: Unravelling the New Capitalism*, Ridley Hall, Cambridge: Grove Books Ltd, 2002.

38. "The John Ray Initiative" is an example of a Christian organization that exists to do just this—see http://www.jri.org.uk.

NOTES FOR CHAPTER 9: CHRISTIANS IN SCIENCE

1. On this point see the books cited in reference 75 of Chapter 5.

2. Letter to Robert Hooke, 5 February 1675/6.

3. 1 Corinthians 12:12–26.

4. See 1 Timothy 6:17–19, where Paul writes that by their generosity and good deeds, the rich will be able to "lay up treasure for themselves as a firm foundation for the coming age."

5. For examples of the way in which riches on earth can hinder riches in heaven, see Mark 10:21, Mark 12:33 and James 5:1–6.

6. Jesus said, "From everyone who has been given much, much will be demanded; and from the one who has been entrusted with much, much more will be asked" (Luke 12:48). See also the parable of the talents in Matthew 25:14–30.

7. See for example Luke 14:25–35.

Index